How to Manage, Analyze, and Interpret Survey Data

2nd edition

THE SURVEY KIT, Second Edition

Purposes: The purposes of this 10-volume Kit are to enable readers to prepare and conduct surveys and to help readers become better users of survey results. Surveys are conducted to collect information; surveyors ask questions of people on the telephone, face-to-face, and by mail. The questions can be about attitudes, beliefs, and behavior as well as socioeconomic and health status. To do a good survey, one must know how to plan and budget for all survey tasks, how to ask questions, how to design the survey (research) project, how to sample respondents, how to collect reliable and valid information, and how to analyze and report the results.

Users: The Kit is for students in undergraduate and graduate classes in the social and health sciences and for individuals in the public and private sectors who are responsible for conducting and using surveys. Its primary goal is to enable users to prepare surveys and collect data that are accurate and useful for primarily practical purposes. Sometimes, these practical purposes overlap with the objectives of scientific research, and so survey researchers will also find the Kit useful.

Format of the Kit: All books in the series contain instructional objectives, exercises and answers, examples of surveys in use and illustrations of survey questions, guidelines for action, checklists of dos and don'ts, and annotated references.

Volumes in The Survey Kit:

1. **The Survey Handbook, 2nd**
   Arlene Fink
2. **How to Ask Survey Questions, 2nd**
   Arlene Fink
3. **How to Conduct Self-Administered and Mail Surveys, 2nd**
   Linda B. Bourque and Eve P. Fielder
4. **How to Conduct Telephone Surveys, 2nd**
   Linda B. Bourque and Eve P. Fielder
5. **How to Conduct In-Person Interviews for Surveys, 2nd**
   Sabine Mertens Oishi
6. **How to Design Survey Studies, 2nd**
   Arlene Fink
7. **How to Sample in Surveys, 2nd**
   Arlene Fink
8. **How to Assess and Interpret Survey Psychometrics, 2nd**
   Mark S. Litwin
9. **How to Manage, Analyze, and Interpret Survey Data, 2nd**
   Arlene Fink
10. **How to Report on Surveys, 2nd**
    Arlene Fink

Arlene Fink

How to Manage, Analyze, and Interpret Survey Data

2nd edition

The Survey Kit 2^{ed}

6 The Survey Kit 2

THE SURVEY KIT
TSK 2

SAGE Publications
International Educational and Professional Publisher
Thousand Oaks ▪ London ▪ New Delhi

For information:

Sage Publications, Inc.
2455 Teller Road
Thousand Oaks, California 91320
E-mail: order@sagepub.com

Sage Publications Ltd.
6 Bonhill Street
London EC2A 4PU
United Kingdom

Sage Publications India Pvt. Ltd.
M-32 Market
Greater Kailash I
New Delhi 110 048 India

Printed in the United States of America

Library of Congress Cataloging-in-Publication Data

The survey kit.—2nd ed.
    p. cm.
Includes bibliographical references.
ISBN 0-7619-2510-4 (set : pbk.)
1. Social surveys. 2. Health surveys. I. Fink, Arlene.
HN29 .S724 2002
300'.723—dc21   2002012405

This book is printed on acid-free paper.

02 03 04 05 10 9 8 7 6 5 4 3 2 1

Acquisitions Editor:	C. Deborah Laughton
Editorial Assistant:	Veronica Novak
Copy Editor:	Judy Selhorst
Production Editor:	Diane S. Foster
Typesetter:	Bramble Books
Proofreader:	Cheryl Rivard
Cover Designer:	Ravi Balasuriya
Production Designer:	Michelle Lee

Contents

How to Manage, Analyze, and Interpret Survey Data: Learning Objectives

A **survey** is a system for collecting information from or about people to describe, compare, or explain their knowledge, attitudes, and behavior. The survey system comprises activities designed to accomplish the collection of valid data; these include setting objectives for information collection, designing the study, preparing a reliable and valid survey instrument, administering the survey, managing and analyzing survey data, and reporting the results.

Survey researchers can collect information directly, by asking people to answer questions, or indirectly, by reviewing written, oral, and visual records of people's thoughts and actions. Surveyors can also obtain data by observing people in natural or experimental settings.

This book has two primary aims: to teach you to how to manage survey data and to help you become better users and consumers of statistical and qualitative survey information. It introduces the basic vocabulary of data management and statistics as well as the principles and logic behind the selection and interpretation of commonly used statistical and qualitative methods for analyzing survey data. What this book does not do is teach you to be a survey statistician. For that, you need to undertake formal study. If you need assistance in choosing or applying any statistical methods, you must obtain a statistician's advice. If this book achieves its objectives, you will be able to tell a statistical consultant or qualitative researcher exactly what you need, and you will be able to interpret the data presented to you.

The specific objectives are to enable you to do the following:

- Organize and manage data for analysis
  - Draft an analysis plan
  - Define and format a data file
  - Create a codebook
  - Establish the reliability of the coding
  - Recognize techniques for dealing with incomplete or missing data and outliers and for recoding

- Identify methods for entering accurate data into spreadsheets, database management programs, and statistical programs

- Learn the use of analytic terms such as the following:
  - Distribution
  - Critical value
  - Skew
  - Transformation
  - Measures of central tendency
  - Dispersion
  - Variation
  - Statistical significance
  - Practical significance
  - p value
  - Alpha
  - Beta
  - Linear
  - Curvilinear
  - Scatterplot
  - Null hypothesis

- List the steps to follow in selecting an appropriate analytic method

- Distinguish among nominal, ordinal, and numerical scales and data so as to:

- Identify independent and dependent variables
- Recognize the appropriate uses of the mean, median, and mode
- Recognize the appropriate uses of the range, standard deviation, percentile rank, and interquartile range
- Understand the logic in and uses of correlations and regression
- Learn the steps in conducting and interpreting hypothesis tests
- Compare and contrast hypothesis testing and the use of confidence intervals
- Calculate the odds ratio and risk ratio
- Understand the logic in and uses of the chi-square distribution and test
- Understand the logic in and uses of the t test
- Understand the logic in and uses of analysis of variance
- Read and interpret computer output

- Understand the basic steps in a content analysis of qualitative data

- Conduct an analysis of open-ended questions asking people what they like least and best

1

Data Management

Data management consists of the activities that survey practioners or surveyors perform to organize survey information so that it can be analyzed. Data management starts with the analysis plan and ends when the data analysis itself begins. Data management activities include the following:

- Drafting an analysis plan
- Creating a codebook
- Establishing reliable coding
- Reviewing surveys for incomplete or missing data
- Entering data and validating the accuracy of the entry
- Cleaning the data

If you plan to do complicated analyses, you will find yourself continuously managing and updating your data to make sure that they are "clean," complete, and appropriate for the analyses you plan to conduct. If your survey is relatively short and involves fewer than about 50 people and 5 variables, you will still have to make sure that the data are

1

clean and complete; you will just spend less time managing your files.

Some surveyors estimate that data management takes between 20% and 50% of the time typically allocated for the analytic process. It is important for you to be realistic about the amount of time you will need for data management and to make sure you have the resources (staff, time, money) to do the job. Below, each of the data management activities is discussed in turn.

Drafting an Analysis Plan

An **analysis plan** describes the analyses you plan to perform for each main survey objective, hypothesis, or research question. Example 1.1 displays a portion of a sample analysis plan.

EXAMPLE 1.1
Portion of an Analysis Plan for a Survey on Children's Exposure to Violence

Survey Objective 1: To compare the numbers of boys and girls who have and have not witnessed violent events at least once a week

Hypothesis: More girls than boys will have witnessed violent events.

Variables: Gender (boys and girls); witness violent acts (yes or no once a week or more)

Planned Analysis: Chi-square to test for differences between numbers of boys and girls who have and have not witnessed violent acts once a week or more

Example 1.1 continued

Survey Objective 2: To compare the scores of boys and girls on the FEAR measure

Research Question: Do differences exist between boys and girls on their scores on the FEAR?

Variables: Gender (boys and girls); average scores (continuous from 1 to 50)

Planned Analysis: t test to test for differences in average FEAR scores obtained by boys and by girls

Survey practioners or surveyors often draft rudimentary analysis plans before they make the final selection of survey items and perform validation of the survey instrument itself. The actualities of deciding what you want to analyze may even dictate the contents of your survey. Funding agencies (such as the National Institutes of Health) and dissertation committees will require you to list your survey's study hypotheses or research questions and to describe how you will analyze data to test each hypothesis or answer each question.

Regardless of how well you plan the analysis, the realities of sampling and data collection may force you to modify your plan. Suppose you are the surveyor whose plan is represented in Example 1.1. You review preliminary FEAR data (Survey Objective 2), and, based on the review, you decide that in addition to testing for differences in average scores, you also want to compare the number of boys and girls who attain scores of 25 or higher on the FEAR to the number who obtain scores of 24 or lower. You would then have to modify your original analysis plan to include a chi-square test as well as the planned *t* test. You should expect to have to make modifications to your original analysis plan, especially in large surveys with a great many data.

Creating a Codebook

Codes are the units or symbols that computer programs use to identify variables. Suppose 1,000 boys and girls complete questionnaires in your survey on violence in school. One question of concern to you is how many boys report being regularly threatened at school. To find out what you want to know on this topic, you have to tell the computer program which survey variables to look for (in this case, sex and threat of violence).

Look at the excerpt from the survey of violence in schools in Example 1.2. The numbers to the right of the boxes that participants use to record their responses are the codes. You can ask a statistical software program to tell you how many people who answered 1 to Question 1 also answered 4 to Question 8. To do this, you must tell the program the names of the variables in which you are interested (Question 1 = **SEX** and Question 8 = **SCHLHURT**) and their values (1 = boy and 4 = almost always). (With many statisti-

EXAMPLE 1.2
Excerpts From a Survey of Violence in Schools

1. Are you a boy or girl? [SEX]

      Boy $\square_1$
      Girl $\square_2$

. . .

8. How often over the past year did anyone **at school** tell you they were going to hurt you? [SCHLHURT]

      Never . . . . $\square_1$
      Sometimes . . . . . . $\square_2$
      Lots of times. . . . . $\square_3$
      Almost always. . . . $\square_4$

cal programs, you also specify where in the data line to find the variables. See the section below on entering the data.)

In Example 1.2, the boldface "words" in brackets (**SEX** and **SCHLHURT**) correspond to the variables represented by the questions. All **codebooks** contain descriptions of the questions, codes, and variables associated with the surveys for which the codebooks were created. A good codebook contains enough information for future researchers to be able to reproduce the survey, the study methods, and the findings. Example 1.3 shows a sample table of contents for a codebook.

EXAMPLE 1.3
Table of Contents for a Codebook

I. **Description of Survey Team**

This section includes a description of the characteristics and experience of the individuals and organizations who are responsible for carrying out the survey.

II. **Methods**

A. *Sampling*

1. *Sampling design* (includes eligibility criteria, e.g., 12 years of age and younger; has read at least three books in the past month)

2. *Sampling strategies* (e.g., stratified random sampling; convenience sampling)

3. *Sample size*

Example 1.3 continued

   4. *Recruitment and enrollment*

   5. *Sampling statistics* (includes weight and sampling error calculations)

   B. *Human subjects:* Informed consent

   C. *Research design* or how participants were assigned to groups (if appropriate); number and timing of survey administration

III. **The Survey**

   A. A copy of the survey and how each response is coded; the variable names associated with each question

   B. Training of data collectors; quality control

   C. Information on reliability and validity

IV. **A Data File Description**

   The variable names (e.g., EDUC), labels (Education), value names and labels (1 = more than 12th grade, 2 = 11th grade or less, 9 = no data)

V. **The Survey Instrument**

   Questions and scoring scheme

You can complete the assembly of the codebook at the conclusion of your survey. At that point, you should also assemble the data file (which some people equate with the codebook) for the analysis. Look at the data file/codebook depicted in Example 1.4. All variables are broken down to discrete units called *values* that correspond to the codes for the variables. For instance, frequency of threats of violence in the school, neighborhood, and elsewhere has four values: 0 = never, 1 = sometimes, 2 = lots of times, and 3 = almost every day. The codes are 0, 1, 2, and 3. If no information is available, a single-digit code is selected to represent that fact, in this case, a 9 (you can also use other single-digit numbers). Also, there are 13 values or codes corresponding to the 13 countries representing respondents' places of birth; in this case, a two-digit code is used for missing data (99). Usually, the codebook lists the variables in the order in which they appear on the survey. The data file may or may not follow that order.

Although statistical software programs vary in terminology, they are fairly consistent in requiring that you name variables using all capital letters (e.g., PQOL or EDUC) and that you avoid the use of special characters, such as commas or semicolons. Some programs limit the number of characters you can use in a name (the maximum is usually about eight). Variable labels are the actual names of the variables (e.g., "perceived quality of life" is the variable label for the variable named PQOL). To understand your data, the statistical program needs to know, for each of your variables, the name (e.g., COMM), the variable label (community), and the value labels and values (urban = 1, rural = 2). (*Please note:* Your program may use slightly different terms, but the ideas will be exactly the same.)

In a large survey project, the codebook is the project's official record. It contains the survey instrument (including the scoring system, if relevant); the variable names, labels, and values or codes; the locations of codes in the data file; information on survey methods, characteristics, and findings; and the names of all survey team members. If you ever

EXAMPLE 1.4
Portions of a Codebook

Variable Name	Variable Label	Values: Labels and Codes
PROJID	Project code	7-digit ID
AGE	Age	Age of student; use 99 for no data
GRADE	Grade	Grade in school: 1-6; use 9 for no data
GENDER	Gender	Gender of respondent: 1 = male, 2 = female; use 9 for no data
CNTRY	Country born in	Country child is born in: 01 = Argentina, 02 = Bolivia, 03 = Chile, 04 = Colombia, 05 = Cuba, 06 = Ecuador, 07 = El Salvador, 08 = Guatemala, 09 = Honduras, 10 = Mexico, 11 = Nicaragua, 12 = Peru, 13 = Puerto Rico; use 99 for no data
SPSPAN	Speak Spanish well	1 = not at all, 2 = a little, 3 = pretty well, 4 = extremely well; use 9 for no data
SPENGLIS	Speak English well	Same as SPSPAN
SCHLHURT	Hurt at school	How often anyone at school told child he/she was going to hurt him/her: 0 = never, 1 = sometimes, 2 = lots of times, 3 = almost every day; use 9 for no data
NEIBHURT	Hurt in neighborhood	How often anyone in neighborhood told child he/she was going to hurt him/her: 0 = never, 1 = sometimes, 2 = lots of times, 3 = almost every day; use 9 for no data
ANYWHERE	Hurt anywhere else	How often anyone anywhere else told child he/she was going to hurt him/her: 0 = never, 1 = sometimes, 2 = lots of times, 3 = almost every day; use 9 for no data

want to use the data from a previous survey (to do additional analyses or even to repeat the survey using a different sample), you will find the original survey's codebook to be essential. You can find sample survey codebooks in their entirety on the Internet by entering the keywords *survey* and *codebook* into your favorite search engine.

Establishing Reliable Coding

If your survey is small, with just one person doing the coding, you can assure the reliability of the data by recoding all or a sample of the data to check for consistency. The second coding should take place about a week after the first; this is enough time for the coder to forget the first set of codes so that he or she does not just automatically reproduce them. After the data are coded a second time, you should compare the two sets of codes for agreement. You can resolve disagreements by calling in a second person to arbitrate.

In large surveys, you should have a second person independently code a sample of the data. To assure reliability between coders, you need to provide the coders with formal training as well as clear definitions of all terms.

Despite your best efforts at setting up a high-quality codebook and data management system, the coders may not always agree with one another. To find out about the extent of their agreement—intercoder or interrater reliability—you can calculate a statistic called **kappa** (κ), which measures how much better than chance the agreement is between a pair of coders.

MEASURING AGREEMENT BETWEEN TWO CODERS: THE KAPPA STATISTIC

Suppose two reviewers are asked to review independently 100 interviews with divorced men who have two or more children. The interviews are about the quality of the men's newly single lives. The reviewers are to study the transcripts of the interviews to find out how many of the men mention their children during the discussion. The reviewers are asked to code 1 for "no," if a man does not mention his children at least once, and 2 for "yes," if he does mention his children. Here are the reviewers' codes:

Reviewer 1

Reviewer 2	No	Yes	
No	20^C	15	35^B
Yes	10	55^D	65
	30^A	70	

Reviewer 1 says that 30 (^{A}) of the 100 interviews do not contain references to the men's children, whereas Reviewer 2 says that 35 (^{B}) do not. The two reviewers agree that 20 (^{C}) interviews do not include mention of the men's children.

What is the best way to describe the extent of agreement between the reviewers? It is probably inaccurate to say 20 of 100 or 20% (^{C}), because the reviewers also agree that 55% (^{D}) of the interviews include mentions of the men's children. The total agreement, 55% + 20%, is an overestimate, because with only two categories (yes and no), some agreement may occur by chance. This is shown in the following formula, in which O is the observed agreement and C is the chance agreement:

$$\kappa = \frac{O - C}{1 - C} \frac{\text{(agreement beyond chance)}}{\text{(agreement possible beyond chance)}}$$

Here is how the formula works with the above example:

1. Calculate how many interviews the reviewers may agree by chance *do not* include mention of the men's children. You do this by multiplying the numbers of nos counted by both reviewers and dividing by 100, because there are 100 interviews: $(30 \_ 35)/100 = 10.5$.

2. Calculate how many interviews the reviewers may agree by chance *do* include mention of the men's children by multiplying the numbers of interviews that both reviewers found to include mention. You do this by multiplying the numbers of yeses counted by both reviewers and dividing by 100: $(70 \times 65)/100 = 45.5$.

3. Add the two numbers obtained in Steps 1 and 2 and divide by 100 to get a proportion for *chance agreement:* $(10.5 + 45.5)/100 = 0.56$.

The *observed agreement* is 20% + 55% = 75%, or 0.75. Therefore the agreement beyond chance is $0.75 - 0.56 = 0.19$; this is the numerator. The *agreement possible beyond chance* is 100% minus the chance agreement of 56%, or $1 - 0.56 = 0.44$; this is the denominator. Thus:

$$\kappa = \frac{0.19}{0.44}$$

$$\kappa = 0.43$$

What is a "high" kappa? Some experts have attached the following qualitative terms to kappas: 0.0-0.2 = slight; 0.2-0.4 = fair; 0.4-0.6 = moderate; 0.6-0.8 = substantial, and 0.8-0.10 = almost perfect.

How do you achieve substantial or almost perfect agreement—reliability—among reviewers? You need to make certain that all reviewers collect and record data on exactly the same topics and that they agree in advance on what each important variable means. The "fair" kappa of 0.43 obtained by the reviewers above can be due to differences between the reviewers' and surveyors' definitions, poor training in the use of the definitions, and mistakes in coding.

Reviewing Surveys for Missing Data

Missing data are the result of unanswered survey questions and lost surveys. You should review the first completed survey instruments as soon as you receive them, before you enter any data, to see if there are problems with missing data. In self-administered, written surveys, especially mailed questionnaires, you can expect to find unanswered questions. Respondents fail to answer questions for a number of reasons: They may not want to answer some kinds of questions, they may simply miss some questions (that is, not see them), or they may not understand certain questions. They may not understand the directions for completing the survey or the questions themselves because the amount of reading they have to do is too great or the reading level is too high. They may be unsure about how they are supposed to respond to some questions (completely fill in the boxes, circle the correct answers, and so on); that is, they may find the question format difficult to understand.

Example 1.5 provides an illustration of a question format that might confuse respondents. In this case, the respondent has answered just one question even though he or she was asked (and reminded) to mark answers on all of the questions. What does the lack of answers on the other items mean? Has the respondent declined to answer the questions because he or she never does the actions described in them? If so, why didn't the respondent mark "never"? In fact, it is not uncommon for respondents to answer only those survey questions they feel are relevant to them. The truth is that the surveyor who created the questionnaire excerpted in Example 1.5 probably used this tabular format to save space and to avoid repeating the response choices over and over. But respondents may find such a format confusing; they are more used to seeing questionnaire items such as that shown in Example 1.6.

Confusing question formats lead to missing data because respondents do not know how to answer the questions. You may be able to avoid some problems that cause respondents

EXAMPLE 1.5
A Question Format That May Be Confusing

Please mark an X through the choice that best describes you.
Please answer each question.

	0	1	2	3
32. How often over the past year have <u>you</u> told others that you would hurt them?	Never	Sometimes	Lots of times	Almost every day
33. How often over the past year have <u>you</u> slapped, punched, or hit someone <u>before</u> that person hit you?	Never	Sometimes	Lots of times	Almost every day
34. How often over the past year have <u>you</u> slapped, hit, or punched someone <u>after</u> that person hit you?	Never	Sometimes	Lots of times	Almost every day
35. How often over the past year have <u>you</u> beaten up someone?	Never	Sometimes	Lots of times	Almost every day
36. How often over the past year have <u>you</u> attacked or stabbed someone with a knife?	Never	Sometimes	Lots of times	Almost every day

DID YOU MARK ONE ANSWER TO EACH
QUESTION EVEN IF YOUR ANSWER IS NEVER?

EXAMPLE 1.6
A Question Format That Is Relatively Easy to Understand

How often over the past year have you attacked or stabbed someone with a knife?

Never . . . . ❏
Sometimes . . . . ❏
Lots of times. . . . . ❏
Almost every day . . . . . ❏

to misunderstand survey questions by conducting extensive cognitive pretests and pilot tests beforehand. Cognitive pretests are interviews with potential respondents in which you ask them to interpret each question and response choice on your survey instrument. Pilot tests are small-scale tests of the survey instrument conducted in the planned survey setting. By conducting these two activities, you can find out before you go to the field if your instrument includes a particular format that is problematic or some questions that do not make sense. But no matter what you do, you can expect some missing data—that is a sure thing!

How to handle missing data is a major problem for survey researchers. Say you mail 100 surveys and get 95 back. You proudly announce that you have a 95% response rate. Upon closer examination, however, you discover that half of the respondents did not answer question 5, and that not a single respondent completed all of the 25 survey questions. With so much information missing, you cannot really claim to have a 95% response rate for all questions.

What should you do about missing responses? In some survey situations, you may be able to go back to the respondents and ask them to answer the questions they neglected.

In small surveys where the respondents are known (say, in an office setting or within a school), you may be able to recontact respondents easily. But collecting missing information by contacting respondents a second time is usually impractical, if not impossible, in most surveys. If your survey is anonymous, you do not even know who the respondents are. In institutional settings, you may need the permission of the institutional review board to contact respondents a second time, a process that takes time and could delay your survey's completion.

Some online surveys take advantage of the capabilities of computer software to prevent respondents from proceeding through a questionnaire without answering all questions in order. Although this can help minimize the problem of missing data, some respondents find the restrictions of these kinds of surveys frustrating, and they may refuse to complete them. Although compelling respondents to answer all questions is touted as a major advantage of computer-assisted surveys, some surveyors believe that forcing respondents to answer every question is coercive and unethical. They argue that participation in most surveys is voluntary, and that respondents should be able to quit when they want to. A computer program that forces people to answer questions even if they prefer not to may be construed by some people as violating the ethical principle of autonomy or respect for individuals. Moreover, such surveys may result in unreliable information, as some people may enter meaningless answers just to be able to move on to the next question.

Entering the Data

Data entry is the process of getting the survey's responses into the computer. It usually takes one of three forms. In the first, someone enters data from the coded survey instruments into a database management or spreadsheet program. The data are then saved as text or ASCII files, so that they can be exported into a statistical program such as SPSS, SAS, or

Stata. A second type of data entry involves entering the data from coded survey instruments directly into a statistical program such as SPSS, SAS, or Stata. In the third form of data entry, the respondent or interviewer enters responses directly into the computer. Data entry of this type is associated with computer-assisted interviewing, Internet surveys, and scanned surveys. The responses are automatically entered into a database management system or statistical programs (usually through special translation software). Programs are also available that will automatically convert one file format into another (say, from SAS to Stata).

Each data entry, database management, and statistical program has its own conventions and terminology. Some programs are set up so that when you enter the data, you set up a "record" for each respondent. The record consists of the person's unique ID (identification code) and the person's "observations" (response choices, scores, comments, and so on). Other programs consider the unit of analysis (such as the person) as the observation, and the data collected on each observation as the variables or fields.

Example 1.7 shows a simple data set for six people. In this example, the table is organized so that, except for the first column, the respondent's identification (RESPID) number constitutes the rows and the data on the respondents are the columns. That is, person 2's data are 2, 4, 1, 3, and 2. Many statistical programs will require you to tell them where on the data line a variable is located. For instance, in Example 1.7, the person's gender is called GENDER, and data on gender can be found in column 2. Violent acts witnessed at home are called VIOLACTH, and the data for this variable can be found in column 5.

Database management programs, statistical programs, and computer-assisted surveys with automatic data entry can facilitate accuracy because they can be programmed to allow the entry of only legal codes. For instance, if the codes that should be entered are 001 through 010, you can write rules so that the program will not permit an entry of 01 or 10 (that is, if you try to enter 01 or 10, you will get an error mes-

EXAMPLE 1.7
Data on Six People

RESPID	GENDER	MARRIED	CHILDREN	VIOLACTH	REPORT
1	1	3	2	1	1
2	2	4	1	3	2
3	2	3	2	3	2
4	1	3	2	1	2
5	1	1	1	1	2
6	1	3	1	3	1

sage). With very little effort, you can also adjust the program to check each entry to ensure that it is consistent with previously entered data and that skip patterns are respected (that is, the program can make sure that the fields for questions that are to be skipped by some respondents are coded as skips and not as missing data). Designing a computer-assisted protocol requires skill and time, and you should never regard any protocol as error-free until it has been tested and retested in the field.

Cleaning the Data

Once the data are entered, they need to be cleaned. If your data set is clean, anyone who uses it will get the same results you do when you run the analysis. Data become "dirty" for a number of reasons, including miscoding, incorrect data entry, and missing responses.

To avoid dirty data, you need to make sure that coders and data enterers are experienced, well trained, and supervised. You should check your variable values against preset maximum and minimum levels, so that if someone enters 50 instead of 5, the maximum, you will know there is an error. You can also minimize errors by making sure your coding scheme distinguishes truly missing (no response or no data) responses from responses of "don't know" or "not applicable."

You should run frequencies (tabulations of the responses to each survey question) on your data as soon as you have about 10% of the responses in, and then run them again and again until you are sure that the survey is running smoothly. If your data set is relatively small, you can visually scan the frequencies for errors. With large databases that have many records, variables, skip patterns, and open-ended text responses, you may need to do systematic computerized checks. All of the leading statistical software programs provide for cleaning specifications that can be used during data entry and later as a separate cleaning process.

Several other problems may require you to clean up the data. These include having to deal with the complete absence of data because some surveys have not been returned, with missing data in surveys that have been returned, and with data in some surveys that are very different from those found in most others.

SOME SURVEYS HAVE NOT BEEN RETURNED

Invariably, some surveys are not going to be returned, regardless of how persuasive you are. If the proportion of nonrespondents is large, you must compare the subjects from whom you have no data against the respondents from whom you have data. You can do this by comparing respondents and nonrespondents in terms of demographic characteristics (age, gender, ethnicity, zip code, and so on), as in Example 1.8. As you can see, the spread of possibilities is large. In fact, low response can ruin a survey.

It is important that you plan to collect data on nonrespondents. If you get a low response rate but you can show that responders and nonresponders are similar, you will

EXAMPLE 1.8
One Way to Deal With Nonresponse

An e-mail survey is conducted to find out whether students are willing to enroll in a new online business course dealing with issues of team building. Surveys are sent to all 100 students in the management program, and 70 students respond. The surveyors are concerned that respondents and nonrespondents differ in age. To account for the 30% nonresponse rate, the surveyors do the following:

1. They calculate the proportions of respondents who are 25 years of age or younger and 26 years of age or older. They estimate that 28 of the 70 students, or 40%, are 25 or under; and 42, or 60%, are 26 or older.

2. They speculate that all 30 nonrespondents are 26 years of age or older, for a total of 30 + 42 or 72 students. That means that 72% may be 26 years old or older, rather than the 60% they had originally calculated.

3. They reason that it is unlikely that all responders are 26 years old and older. Some must be 25 or younger. But how many? To solve the mystery, they telephone a random sample of 10 nonresponders and find that 7 are 25 or younger. They then use the following formula, which calculates the 95% confidence limits of a point (in this case, the percentage) estimate:

P (the true proportion of students 25 years or younger) $= 1.96 \times \left(\sqrt{PQ/n} \right)$

Example 1.8 continued

or

$$1.96 \times \left(\sqrt{(.7)(.3)/10}\right) = .28$$

The probable answer for the 10 nonresponders is .70 – .28. Somewhere between 41% and 98% of the 30 nonresponders are 26 years old and older. The surveyors can now guess that 42 (the responders who are 26 years of age and older) plus 17 to 30 students are 26 years old or older. This means that between 59% (17 + 42) and 72% (42 + 72) are in the older age group.

strengthen your justification for accepting the survey's findings as legitimate. You might have to be ingenious when making the comparison. In an anonymous mailed survey, for example, you can compare responders and nonresponders by zip code. In an e-mail survey, you can compare the numbers of returned and nonreturned surveys from ".com" or ".net" addresses with the numbers from ".org" or ".edu" addresses.

To minimize low response rates, you should make sure that your survey is meaningful to the intended responders. Is the topic important enough so that they feel compelled to answer the questions? Be sure to respect the rules of confidentiality. Check the survey's readability level, format, and aptness of the language through cognitive pretesting and scientific translation. If the reading level is too high, or the format is cluttered, or the translation is poor (any one of these will do), then you can count on people to ignore the survey. If your survey is going to be administered by interviewers, spend the time and money to train them well beforehand, and then continue to monitor their work once interviewing begins. You can lose respondents if they do not understand or like the people interviewing them. It sometimes helps to offer respondents financial or other incentives (such as gifts or gift certificates) to complete your survey. Follow up with respondents through e-mail, by conventional mail, and/or by telephone.

Survey researchers often use a statistical method called **weighting** to make up for nonresponse. For example, if you expect that your survey will be completed by a sample made up of 50% men and 50% women, but only 40% of the completed surveys are returned by men, you can weight the men's returns so that they are equivalent to 50%. There are several strategies for accomplishing this, among them logistic regression analysis. The existence or nonexistence of a response is considered a dichotomous dependent variable and other variables are used to predict it. Dichotomous variables are divided into two components. For instance, if the variable age is dichotomous, then it is divided into two parts, such as 65 and older, and 64 and younger. Scores can be dichotomized: 50 and under, and 51 and older. Practically any variable can be dichotomized or divided into two parts.

Suppose you have information on age and gender, *and* you can predict whether or not a person responded using these two variables—that is, your respondents and nonrespondents differ on these characteristics. Logistic regression provides you with an estimate of the probability that a given respondent's data will be missing. The probabilities are assigned as weights for all cases. Cases that have missing data are given higher weights. All statistical software programs include mechanisms for weighting responses.

SOME RETURNED SURVEYS HAVE DATA MISSING

Survey researchers often use statistical **imputation** to deal with missing data; that is, they impute or estimate how respondents who did not answer particular questions would have answered them if they had chosen to. Suppose you are conducting a survey to find out about the effects of a major flood. One of the questions concerns the amount of money the respondents needed to repair the damage on their homes. After reviewing the returned surveys, you realize that about 15 people did not answer this question. Further review reveals that the question itself was missing from some of the questionnaires. One way in which you might estimate what those 15 people would have reported, had they answered the question, is to identify others in the sample whose homes had similar damage, compute the average costs, and assign those averages to the 15 nonresponders.

Researchers tend to have mixed feelings about imputation. Little consensus is available about the validity of results arrived at in this way. If you choose to impute, you should consider analyzing the data both with and without the missing values replaced and then comparing the results to make certain that the method of replacement does not lead to a very different interpretation of the data than you would have come to otherwise.

SOME PEOPLE ARE OUTLIERS

Outliers are respondents whose answers appear to be inconsistent with the rest of the data set. You can detect them by using your statistical program's built-in checks or by running frequencies and other descriptive statistics and checking the results against acceptable values. For instance, suppose you survey 50 people to find out if they like a particular movie. You review the returns and find that 48 respondents have assigned ratings of 2, 3, and 4 on a scale of 1 (*hated it*) to 5 (*loved it*). One respondent has been consistently negative and has assigned ratings of 1 to all 75 questions about the movie. One other respondent has assigned ratings of 5 to all 75 questions. These two people may be outliers—the question is what to do about them.

Many researchers simply discard outliers from the data analysis. You must decide on a case-by-case basis what you should do with data that clearly deviate from the norm. Be cautious: When you discard seemingly deviant data, you may also be tossing out important information. Methods of detecting outliers include regression analysis and formal tests that assume that variables are normally distributed. (See Chapter 3 for a discussion of the normal distribution.)

SOME DATA NEED TO BE RECODED

The process of data management may continue until the last analysis has been performed. For example, as time goes on, you may want to add some people to the survey sample, or you may want to add variables. These activities will require more data coding, entry, and cleaning. You may need to recode the data you have collected, as illustrated in Example 1.9.

EXAMPLE 1.9
Recoding Data

Recoding Survey 1

In a survey of people's attitudes toward reports of global warming, the interviewers collect data on age by asking for birth date. Preliminary analysis reveals that respondents' ages range from age 18 to 97. The median age of the sample is 42. The survey team decides to compare the attitudes of older and younger people, so they recode the data to make two age categories: 42 years old and younger, and 43 years old and older.

Recoding Survey 2

For a survey concerning family life, the survey team adopts a standardized measure of family stability. The measure has 10 items, each rated on a scale of 1 to 5. The survey team discovers, however, that 7 of the items are worded so that a score of 1 is high and a score of 5 is low. On the other 3 items, a score of 5 is high and a score of 1

Example 1.9 continued

is low. Because the surveyors want a total score of family stability, they have to recode the three reverse-worded questions so that a 1 is scored as if it were a 5, a 2 as if it were a 4, and so on. If they do not recode the data, the items will not have a common direction, and they will be unable to sum the items to get a score.

2 What Statistics Do for Surveys

Statistics is the mathematics of organizing and interpreting numerical information. The results of statistical analyses are descriptions, relationships, comparisons, and predictions, as shown in Example 2.1. In the first of the illustrative results in the example, the findings are tallied and reported as percentages. A tally, or frequency count, is a computation of how many people fit into a category (men or women, under or over 70 years of age, read five or more books last year or did not). Tallies and frequencies take the form of numbers and percentages.

EXAMPLE 2.1
Statistical Analysis and Survey Data

A researcher surveys 160 people to find out about the numbers and types of books they read. The researcher then analyzes the respondents' answers statistically to do the following:

Example 2.1 continued

- Describe the backgrounds of the respondents
- Describe the responses to each of the questions
- Determine if a connection exists between the number of books a person has read and his or her travel during the past year
- Compare the number of books read by men with the number read by women
- Find out if gender, education, or income predicts how frequently the respondents read books

The following are some illustrative results:

1. *Describe respondents' backgrounds.* Of the survey's 160 respondents, 77 (48.1%) were men, with 72 (48%) earning more than $50,000 per year and having at least 2 years of college. Of the 150 respondents answering the question, 32 (21.3%) stated that they always or nearly always read for pleasure.

2. *Describe responses.* Respondents were asked how many books they read in a year and whether they prefer fiction or nonfiction. On average, college graduates read 10 or more books, with a range of 2 to 50. The typical college graduate prefers nonfiction to fiction.

3. *Relationship between travel and number of books read.* Respondents were asked how often they traveled in the past year, and frequency of travel was compared to number of books read. Respondents who traveled at least twice in the past year read five or more books.

Example 2.1 continued

4. *Comparisons.* The percentages of men and women who read five or more books each year were compared, and no differences were found. On average, women's reading attitude scores were statistically significantly higher and more positive than men's, but older men's scores were significantly higher than older women's.

5. *Predicting frequency.* Education and income were found to be the best predictors of frequency of reading. That is, respondents with the most education and income read the most (one or more books each week).

In the second sample of results shown in Example 2.1, the findings are presented as averages ("on average," "the typical" reader). When you are interested in the center (e.g., the average) of a distribution of findings, you are concerned with measures of central tendency. Measures of dispersion or spread, such as the range, are often given along with measures of central tendency.

In the third example of results in Example 2.1, the survey reports on the relationship between traveling and number of books read. One way of estimating the relationship between two characteristics is through correlation.

In the fourth example, comparisons are made between men and women. The term *statistical significance* is used; this means that the differences that have been found are statistically meaningful and are not explainable by chance alone.

In the fifth example, survey data are used to "predict" frequent reading. In simpler terms, using data in this way means answering questions such as the following: Of all the characteristics on which survey data are available (e.g., income, education, type of books read, travel and leisure preferences), which one or ones are linked to frequent reading? For instance, does income make a difference? Education? Income and education?

What methods should you use to describe, summarize, compare, and predict? Before you can answer that question, you must answer at least four others:

- Do the survey data come from nominal, ordinal, or numerical scales or measures?

- How many independent and dependent variables are there?

- What statistical methods are potentially appropriate?

- Do the survey data fit the requirements of the methods?

Measurement Scales:
Nominal, Ordinal, and Numerical

A characteristic may be surveyed and measured using nominal, ordinal, or numerical scales, and the resulting data are termed nominal, ordinal, or numerical.

NOMINAL SCALES

Nominal scales have no numerical value and produce data that fit into categories, such as country of birth or gender. Nominal scales and the data they yield are sometimes called *categorical scales* and *categorical data*. Example 2.2 displays two typical kinds of survey questions that result in nominal or categorical data. For both questions, the answer is the "name" of the category into which the data fit. The numbers are arbitrary and have no inherent value. In Question 1, for instance, "female" could be labeled 1 and "male" 2. The numbers are merely codes. When nominal data take on one of two values, as in Question 1 in Example 2.2 (e.g., male or female), they are termed **dichotomous**.

EXAMPLE 2.2
Survey Questions That Use
Nominal Scales and Produce Nominal Data

What is the employee's gender? *Circle one.*

Male	1
Female	2

Describe the type of lung cancer. *Circle one.*

Small cell	1
Large cell	2
Oat cell	3
Squamous cell	4

ORDINAL SCALES

If an inherent order exists among the categories, the data are said to have been obtained from an **ordinal scale**, as illustrated in Example 2.3. Ordinal scales typically are seen in questions that call for ratings of quality (e.g., excellent, very good, good, fair, poor, very poor) or agreement (e.g., strongly agree, agree, disagree, strongly disagree).

NUMERICAL (INTERVAL AND RATIO) SCALES

When differences between numbers have a meaning on a **numerical scale**, the data are called numerical. Age is a numerical variable, as are weight and length of survival after diagnosis of a serious disease. Numerical data lend themselves to precision; for example, you can obtain data on age to the nearest second.

EXAMPLE 2.3
Survey Questions That Use Ordinal Scales

1. How much education have you completed? *Circle one.*

Never finished high school	1
High school graduate but no college	2
Some college	3
College graduate	4

2. Stage of tumor? *Circle one.*

Duke's A	1
Duke's B	2
Duke's C	3
Duke's D	4

3. How often during the past month did you find yourself having difficulty trying to calm down? *Circle one.*

Always	5
Very often	4
Fairly often	3
Sometimes	2
Almost never	1

You may also hear the terms *interval scales* and *ratio scales*. Interval scales have an arbitrary zero point; examples include the Fahrenheit and Celsius temperature scales. The difference, or distance, between 40° and 50°Celsius is the same as the difference between 70° and 80°, but 40° is not twice as hot as 20°, and 0° does not mean no temperature at all. Ratio scales, in contrast, have a true zero point, as in the absolute zero value of the Kelvin scale. Practically speaking, ratio scales are extremely rare, and statistically, interval and ratio scales are treated the same; hence, the term *numerical* is a more apt (and neutral) label.

Numerical data can be continuous (e.g., height, weight, age) or discrete (e.g., numbers of visits to a clinic, numbers of previous pregnancies). Survey researchers use means and standard deviations to summarize the values of numerical measures. The three kinds of measurement scales and their data types are contrasted in Table 2.1.

Independent and Dependent Variables

A **variable** is a characteristic that is measurable. Weight is a variable, and all persons weighing 55 kilograms have the same numerical weight. Satisfaction with a product is also a variable, but in the case of this kind of variable, a numerical scale has to be devised and rules must be created for its interpretation. For example, in Survey A, product satisfaction is measured on a scale from 1 to 100, with 100 representing perfect satisfaction. Survey B, however, measures satisfaction by counting the number of repeat customers. The rule is that satisfaction is demonstrated when at least 15% of all customers reorder the product within a year.

Your choice of method for analyzing survey data will always be dependent on the type of data available to you (nominal, ordinal, and numerical) and on the number of dependent and independent variables involved.

Independent variables are also called *explanatory* or *predictor* variables, because they are used to explain or predict a response, outcome, or result—the **dependent variable.** You can identify the independent and dependent variables in a survey by studying the survey's objectives and target. In Example 2.4, for instance, Survey 1 has three independent variables and one dependent variable; Survey 2 has three independent and two dependent variables. The next step in the analytic process is to determine whether the survey's data for these variables are nominal, ordinal, or numerical (see Example 2.5).

TABLE 2.1   Nominal, Ordinal, and Numerical Measurement Scales:
Examples, Features, and Comments

Measurement Scale and Type of Data	Examples	Features/Comments
Nominal	Type of disease (small-cell, large-cell, oat-cell, or squamous-cell cancer); grade in school (9th, 10th, 11th, or 12th); ethnicity; gender	Observations belong to categories. Observations have no inherent order of importance. Observations sometimes are called *categorical*.
Ordinal	Ratings of quality (excellent, very good, good, fair, poor) or of agreement (strongly agree, agree, disagree, strongly disagree); rankings (the top 10 movies)	Order exists among the categories—that is, one observation is of greater value than the other or more important.
Numerical	Continuous numerical scales: scores on an achievement test or attitude inventory; age; height; length of survival Discrete numerical scales: number of visits to a physician; number of falls; number of days absent from work or class	Differences between numbers have meaning (e.g., higher scores mean better achievement than lower scores, and a difference between 12 and 13 has the same meaning as a difference between 99 and 100). Some statisticians distinguish between interval scales (arbitrary 0 point, as in the Fahrenheit scale) and ratio scales (absolute 0, as in the Kelvin scale); these measures are usually treated the same statistically, so they are combined here as numerical.

When you set out to choose an appropriate analysis method, you should begin by deciding on the purpose of the analysis. You can then determine the number of independent and dependent variables and whether you have nomi-

EXAMPLE 2.4
Targets and Independent Variables

Survey 1

Objective: To describe the quality of life of men over 65 years of age with different health characteristics (e.g., whether or not they have hypertension or diabetes) and social backgrounds (e.g., whether they live alone or live with someone; whether they are employed or unemployed). The men in the survey had surgery for prostate cancer within the past 2 years.

Target: Men over 65 years of age with differing health characteristics and social backgrounds who have had surgery for prostate cancer within the past 2 years

Independent Variables: Age (over 65 years of age), health characteristics (presence or absence of hypertension or diabetes), and social background (living alone or not and employment status)

Dependent Variable: Quality of life

Survey 2

Objective: To compare elementary school children in different grades in two ways: (a) opinions on the school's new dress code and (b) attitudes toward school

Target: Boys and girls in grades 3 through 6 in five elementary schools

Independent Variables: Gender, grade level, and school

Dependent Variables: Opinion of new dress code and attitude toward school

EXAMPLE 2.5
Are Data Nominal, Ordinal, or Numerical?

Survey 1: Men With Prostate Cancer

Independent Variables

- Age (over 65 years of age)

- Health characteristics (presence or absence of hypertension or diabetes)

- Social background (whether living alone or not and employment status)

Characteristics of Survey Questions

- To get age, ask for exact birth date.

- To find out about health characteristics, ask, "Do you have any of the following medical conditions? Answer yes or no for each."

- To find out about social background, ask respondents to answer yes or no regarding whether or not they live alone and are currently employed full-time, employed part-time, or not employed at all.

Type of Data

- Age: Numerical (birth date)

- Health characteristics: Nominal (presence or absence of medical conditions)

- Social background: Nominal (live alone or do not; employed or not)

Dependent Variable

- Quality of life

Example 2.5 continued

Characteristics of Survey Questions

- Ask questions that call for ratings of various aspects of quality of life. For example, ask respondents to describe how frequently they feel restless, down in the dumps, rattled, moody, and so on.

- Use categories for the responses, such as "all of the time," "most of the time," "a good bit of the time," "some of the time," "a little of the time," "none of the time."

Type of Data

- Quality of life: Ordinal (may be numerical if statistical evidence exists that higher scores are statistically and practically different from lower scores)

Survey 2: Children, Dress Code, and Attitude Toward School

Independent Variables

- Gender

- Grade level

- Schools

Characteristics of Survey Questions

- To get gender, ask if male or female.

- Ask participants to write in grade level and name of school.

Type of Data

- Gender: Nominal

- Grade level: Nominal

- Name of school: Nominal

Example 2.5 continued

Dependent Variables

- Opinion of new dress code
- Attitude toward school

Characteristics of Survey Questions

- To get opinions on the new dress code, ask for ratings of like and dislike (e.g., from "like a lot" to "dislike a lot").

- To learn about attitudes, use the Attitude Toward School Rating Scale.

Type of Data

- Opinions of dress code: Ordinal
- Attitudes: Ordinal

nal, ordinal, or numerical data. Example 2.6 shows how this process works in two hypothetical cases (the two statistical methods mentioned in the example are discussed later). In this example, both of the choices of analytic method are labeled "possible." The appropriateness of your choice of a statistical method depends on the method's *assumptions* about the characteristics and quality of the data. In the two cases in Example 2.6, too little information is given for us to know whether or not the assumptions are met.

The discussion that follows is intended to help you understand the logic behind the choice of an analytic method. Some of the most commonly accepted statistical procedures and their assumptions are described, and example of formulas are presented. This material is offered not to turn you into a survey statistician but to guide you in obtaining the information you need to choose the correct method

EXAMPLE 2.6
Choosing an Analysis Method

Survey Objective: To compare scores on the Quality of Life Inventory achieved by men who are employed full-time, employed part-time, or unemployed and who had surgery for prostate cancer 2 years ago.

Number of Independent Variables: One (employment status)

Type of data: Nominal (employed full-time, employed part-time, unemployed)

Number of Dependent Variables: One (quality of life)

Type of data: Numerical (scores)

Name of Possible Method of Analysis: One-way analysis of variance

Survey Objective: To compare boys and girls with differing scores on the Attitude Toward School Questionnaire in terms of whether they do or do not support the school's new dress code

Number of Independent Variables: One (gender)

Type of data: Nominal (boys, girls)

Number of Dependent Variables: One (support dress code)

Type of data: Nominal (support, do not support)

Possible Method of Analysis: Logistic regression

of analysis for your survey. When you implement your analysis, the calculations will be meaningful only if they are the ones you need and the data are available and clean.

You should complete the activities on the following checklist *before* you choose an analysis method.

Checklist for Choosing a Method to Analyze Survey Data

✓ Count the number of independent variables.

✓ Determine whether the data on the independent variables are nominal, ordinal, or numerical.

✓ Count the number of dependent variables.

✓ Determine whether the data on the dependent variables are nominal, ordinal, or numerical.

✓ Choose potential data-analytic methods.

✓ Screen the survey's objectives (description, relationship, prediction, comparison) against the analysis method's assumptions and outcomes.

Descriptive Statistics and Measures of Central Tendency: Numerical and Ordinal Data

Descriptive statistics describe data in terms of **measures of central tendency.** These are measures or statistics that describe the location of the center of a **distribution,** or an arrangement of data that shows the frequency of occurrence of the values (e.g., scores and other numerical values, such as number of years in office, age in years as of today) of a variable or characteristic (e.g., attitudes, knowledge, behavior, health status, and demographics, such as age and income). For example, in a survey that asks respondents if they are under 25 years of age or 25 years old or older, the distribution is formed by the ages (with the values, under 25 years and 25 years and older) and the frequency (the number of respondents in each of the two age categories). In a survey that produces scores on a scale from 1 to 10, the distribution of scores consists of the numbers of people who achieve scores of 1, 2, and so on up to scores of 10. The three measures of central tendency are the mean, median, and mode; each is discussed in turn in the subsections below.

Measures of dispersion are descriptive statistics that depict the spread of numerical data. For example, in a survey that produces scores on a scale from 1 to 10, you calculate measures of dispersion to answer questions like "Are most of the scores clustered around a single score, say, 5?" and "What is the highest score? The lowest?" There are four kinds of measures of dispersion (or spread): the range, the standard deviation, percentiles, and the interquartile range. Each of these is discussed later in this chapter, in the section on measures of spread.

MEAN

The **mean** (which is symbolized as $\bar{X}$) is the arithmetic average of observations. To calculate the mean, you divide the total numerical values of the observations (scores or responses) by the number of observations.

The formula for calculating the mean is $\Sigma X/n$. Σ, the capital Greek letter sigma, indicates to add or sum. X is each individual observation, and n is the total number of observations. Example 2.7 shows the calculation of the mean.

Suppose the 15th student in Example 2.7 had obtained a score of 20 rather than 6. In that case, the mean would be 39/15, or 2.6. The mean is sensitive to extreme values in a set of observations.

You can use the mean as your measure of central tendency only when the numbers you have can be added or when characteristics are measured on a numerical scale, such as the kinds of scales used to describe height, weight, and scores on a test.

EXAMPLE 2.7
Calculating the Mean

Students who took the 20-point Attitude Toward Spelling Survey received these 15 scores:

$$-6, -3, -3, 0, 2, 2, 2, 3, 3, 3, 3, 4, 4, 5, 6$$

The mean ($\Sigma X/n$) of the scores is calculated as follows. First, the scores themselves are totaled:

$$(-6) + (-3) + (-3) + (0) + (2) + (2) + (2) + (3) + (3) + (3) + (3) + (4) + (4) + (5) + (6) = 25$$

The result is then divided by the total number of scores:

$$25/15 = 1.67$$

MEDIAN

The **median** is the middle observation—that is, half of the observations are smaller than the median and half are larger. Because it falls in the middle, the median is sometimes considered the "typical" observation.

To determine the median, you need to take the following steps:

1. Arrange the observations (scores, responses) from lowest to highest (or vice versa).

2. Count to the middle value. If you have an odd number of observations, the median is the middle value; if you have an even number of observations, the median is the mean of the two values that fall in the middle of the arranged observations.

Consider this odd number of scores:

$$3, 6, 6, 7, 9, 13, 17$$

In this case, the median is 7, because half of the scores (3, 6, 6) are below that point and half (9, 13, 17) are above it. Now suppose you have the following even number of scores:

$$-2, 0, 6, 7, 9, 9$$

The two middle scores in this sequence are 6 and 7, so to get the median for these scores, you add 6 + 7 and divide by 2, for a result of 6.5.

EXERCISES

1. Calculate the median for the following scores:

$$2, 4, 5, 8, 9, 11$$

2. Calculate the median for the following scores:

$$3, 9, 7, -2, 6, 7$$

• •
ANSWERS

1. The median is 6.5.

2. The median is 6.5. (To calculate it, you must first rearrange the scores so that you have 9, 7, 7, 6, 3, –2, or –2, 3, 6, 7, 7, 9.)

The median is not as sensitive as the mean to extreme values, so if you have a few outliers in the distribution, you will probably want to use the median rather than the mean.

MODE

The **mode of a distribution** is the value of the observations that occurs most frequently. Researchers commonly use the mode when they want to show the most "popular" value. Example 2.8 shows samples of two kinds of modes of distribution. Distribution A has a single mode of 29, with 18 responses. This distribution is *unimodal*. Distribution B has two modes, at 25 and 31, so the distribution is *bimodal*.

EXAMPLE 2.8
Sample Unimodal and Bimodal Distributions

Distribution A		Distribution B	
Score	Frequency	Score	Frequency
34	2	34	0
33	6	33	1
32	8	32	7
31	11	31	21
30	15	30	4
29	18	29	3
28	10	28	7
27	12	27	10
26	8	26	14
25	3	25	23
24	1	24	11
23	0	23	5

Distributions: Skewed and Symmetric

A distribution that has a few outlying observations in one direction—a few small values or a few large ones—is called a **skewed distribution.** A **symmetric distribution** is a distribution that has the same shape on both sides of the mean. Figure 2.1 shows that if the mean and median are equal, the distribution of observations is symmetric (A). If the mean is smaller than the median, the distribution is skewed to the left (B). If the mean is larger than the median, the distribution is skewed to the right (C).

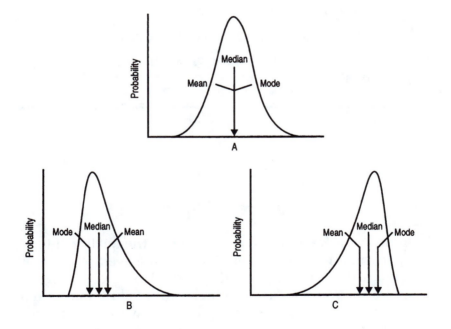

Figure 2.1. Distributions: Skewed and Symmetric

Checklist: When to Use the Mean, Median, and Mode

✓ Use the *mean* when

- The distribution is approximately symmetric.
- You are interested in numerical values.

✓ Use the *median* when

- You are concerned with the typical score.
- The distribution is skewed.
- You have ordinal data.

✓ Use the *mode* when

- The distribution has two or more peaks.
- You want the prevailing view, characteristic, or quality.

Measures of Spread

Suppose you ask a group of people to rate the quality of food at a particular restaurant. You find that the average rating is 3.5 on a scale of 1 (*poor*) to 5 (*excellent*). How close in agreement are the respondents? Do their ratings cluster around 3 (the middle point), or are they spread out, with some people assigning ratings of 1 and some giving ratings of 5? There are four ways to express the extent of the spread (also called *dispersion* or *variation*) of observations: the range, the standard deviation, percentiles, and the interquartile range.

RANGE

The **range** is the difference between the largest observation and the smallest. Sometimes, the range is expressed by highest and lowest values rather than just the difference between them. Example 2.9 demonstrates how the range is used.

EXAMPLE 2.9
Using the Range

The following are the scores achieved by 10 people on the 20-item Survey of Compassionate Behavior:

4, 7, 9, 11, 11, 12, 14, 16, 17, 18

The scores range from 4 to 18; thus, the range is 14 points.

STANDARD DEVIATION

The **standard deviation** (*SD*) is a measure of the spread of the data around the mean; it is an essential part of many statistical tests. Although it is highly unlikely that you will ever need to compute a standard deviation "by hand," you may find it useful to understand how the standard deviation functions.

Calculation of the standard deviation depends on the calculation of the average distance from the mean of the average score. The definitional formula is as follows:

$$SD = \sqrt{\sum(X - \overline{X})^2 / (n - 1)}$$

Suppose you had the following 10 scores on the Survey of Compassionate Behavior:

$$7, 10, 8, 5, 4, 8, 4, 9, 7, 8$$

Here is how you would calculate the standard deviation:

- Compute the mean:
1. $\bar{X} = (7 + 10 + 8 + 5 + 4 + 8 + 4 + 9 + 7 + 8)/10 = 7$.
2. Subtract the mean $(\bar{X})$ from each score (X), or $X - \bar{X}$.
3. Square each remainder from Step 2, or $(X - \bar{X})^2$.

Score	Step 2 $(X - \bar{X})$	Step 3 $(X - \bar{X})^2$
7	$(7 - 7) = 0$	0
10	$(10 - 7) = 3$	9
8	$(8 - 7) = 1$	1
5	$(5 - 7) = -2$	4
4	$(4 - 7) = -3$	9
8	$(8 - 7) = 1$	1
4	$(4 - 7) = -3$	9
9	$(9 - 7) = 2$	4
7	$(7 - 7) = 0$	0
8	$(8 - 7) = 1$	1

4. Sum (Σ) all the squares from Step 3, or $\Sigma(X - \bar{X})^2$:

$$\Sigma(X - \bar{X})^2 = 0 + 9 + 1 + 4 + 9 + 1 + 9 + 4 + 0 + 1 = 38.$$

5. Divide the number in Step 4 by $n - 1$:

$$38/(n - 1) = 38/9 = 4.22.$$

A digression: n is the number of scores; $n - 1$ is used because it produces a more accurate estimate of the true population's standard deviation and has other desirable mathematical properties. The quantity $n - 1$ is called the *degrees of freedom,* a concept that appears in other statistical formulas and tables. (The term *degrees of freedom* sounds intuitively mean-ingful, but this concept is in fact quite complex and well beyond the scope of this book; it is discussed in advanced texts concerned with the principles of statistics.)

6. Take the square root of the result of Step 5:

$$\sqrt{4.2} = 2.05.$$

The standard deviation squared is called the *variance*. In the above example, the variance is 4.22. This statistic is not used as often as the standard deviation, which has two character-istics that you should keep in mind:

- Regardless of how the survey observations are distrib-uted, at least 75% of them will always fall between the mean plus 2 standard deviations ($\overline{X} + 2SD$) and the mean minus 2 standard deviations ($\overline{X} - 2SD$). Suppose the mean of 32 scores is 12 and the standard deviation is 1.2. At least 75% of the 32 scores, or 24 scores, will be between $12 + (2 \times 1.2)$ and $12 - (2 \times 1.2)$, or between 14.4 and 9.6.

- If the distribution of the scores is symmetric (bell-shaped or normal), as shown in Figure 2.2, the follow-ing rules apply:

  About 68% of all observations fall between the mean and 1 standard deviation.

  About 95% of all observations fall between the mean and 2 standard deviations.

  About 99% of all observations fall between the mean and 3 standard deviations.

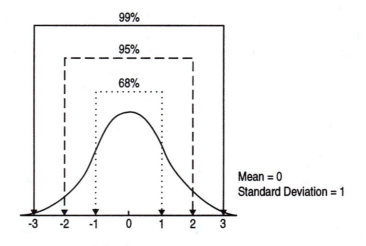

Figure 2.2.   Normal Distribution

PERCENTILE

A **percentile** is a number that indicates the percentage of a distribution that is equal to or below that number. To say that a person scored in the 95th percentile means that 95% of others scored the same as or lower than that person. Percentiles are often used in comparisons of individual values with particular sets of standards. If a school's reading scores on standardized tests are in the 30th percentile, for example, this indicates where the school stands in relation to a standard or norm such as statewide scores; in this case, 30% of other schools have the same or lower scores and 70% have the same or higher scores. The median is the 50th percentile; that is, half of the distribution is at or above that point, and half is at or below it.

INTERQUARTILE RANGE

A measure of variation that makes use of percentiles is the **interquartile range,** which is the difference between the 25th and the 75th percentiles. The interquartile range contains the 50% of the observations that fall in the middle of the full range. For example, suppose students at the 25th percentile have an average score of 30.2, and those at the 75th have a score of 90.1. The central 50% of the scores, or the interquartile range, is the difference between 90.1 (the 75th percentile) and 30.2 (the 25th). Another way to put it is that 50% of the students achieved scores between 30.2 and 90.1.

Guidelines for Selecting Measures of Dispersion

- *Range.* Numerical (e.g., scores from 1 to 100). The range describes the highest and lowest scores.

- *Standard deviation.* Numerical. Standard deviations describe the spread of means.

- *Percentile.* Ordinal (e.g., ratings on a scale from 1 = *very bad* to 5 = *very good*) or numerical (e.g., scores). The median is the 50th percentile.

- *Interquartile range.* Ordinal or numerical. The interquartile range is the central 50% of a set of observations, or the difference between the 75th and the 25th percentiles.

Descriptive Statistics and Nominal Data

Survey characteristics that are measured on a nominal scale do not have numerical values, but you can count them and describe how frequently they occur. The following are typical of the kinds of survey questions that produce nominal data:

Did you read these books?
Jane Eyre	Yes	No
Schindler's List	Yes	No

Which best describes your current living status? *Circle one only.*

Living alone	Yes	No
Living with a friend, not related	Yes	No
Living with a relative	Yes	No
Living in a communal arrangement	Yes	No
Other (specify _____)	Yes	No

For each question and its component parts, the response choice is yes or no: Yes, I read *Jane Eyre,* or no, I did not; yes, I live alone, or no, I do not; and so on. Survey researchers analyze nominal survey data by using descriptive statistics such as proportion, percentage, ratio, and rate.

PROPORTION AND PERCENTAGE

A statement of **proportion** is an expression of the number of observations or responses with a given characteristic divided by the total number of observations. Put another way, proportion is the relation of a *part* to the *whole*. For example, the data in Table 2.2 show that the number of respondents in the experimental group who felt better is 65; divide that number by the total number of responses in the experimental group (better and worse), which is 69, and you get the proportion of those who felt better in the experimental group: 65/69, or .9420. In the control group, the proportion who felt better is 73/83, or .8795.

A **percentage** is a form of proportion in which the part of the whole is expressed in hundredths. Thus, to convert a proportion to a percentage, you multiply by 100. Extending the example above, 94.2% (.9420 × 100) of those in the experimental group felt better, and 87.9% (.8795 ×100) of those in the control group did also.

The proportion is a special case of the mean in which the observations with a given characteristic (say, people who felt better) are assigned the value 1 and the observations without the characteristic or with the opposite characteristic (say, people who felt worse) are assigned the value 0. The sum X

TABLE 2.2   Perceptions of Members of Experimental and Control Groups

Outcome	Experimental Group	Control Group
Felt better	65	73
Felt worse	4	10
Total	69	83

in the numerator of the formula for the mean is the sum of the 0s and 1s, and the denominator is still n (the number of observations). So, using the data from Table 2.2, the proportion of people who felt better is $[(65 \times 1) + (4 \times 0)]/69$, or .9420.

RATIO AND RATE

A **ratio** is the relationship of one *part* of the whole to another *part*, expressed as a part divided by another part. It is the number of observations in a given group with a certain characteristic (e.g., feeling better) divided by the number of observations without the given characteristic (e.g., feeling worse). Using the data in Table 2.2, the ratio of feeling better to feeling worse in the experimental group is 65/4, or 16.25. The ratio of feeling better to feeling worse in the control group is 73/10, or 7.3.

A **rate** is a form of proportion measured per unit of some multiplier or base, such as 1,000, 10,000, or 100,000. Rates are always computed over time (e.g., over the course of a year). Using the data in Table 2.2, suppose the experimental group participated in the study for a year, and the base for the rate of feeling better was set at 1,000. The rate of feeling better per 1,000 persons per year is then $(65/69) \times 1,000$, or about 942 persons for each 1,000 per year.

3 Relationships and Comparisons

Numerical Data

A **relationship** is a consistent association between or among variables. The following questions, from four different survey studies, are all about relationships:

1. Are the readers of this magazine also financially well off?

2. Do children who visit the school nurse most often have low self-concepts?

3. Do two observers agree on what they see?

4. Do people who do well in the program read well?

The relationship of interest in Question 1 is that between readers and financial well-being. Question 2 seeks information about the relationship between frequency of visits to the school nurse and self-concept; Question 3, about the relationship between what Observers 1 and 2 see; and Question 4, about the relationship between success in the program and high reading ability.

When you are concerned with discovering the relationship between two variables, you are ready for **correlation analysis.** When the two variables are expressed numerically, you use a correlation coefficient, sometimes called a *Pearson product-moment coefficient* (after the statistician who discovered it). The correlation coefficient has a range of +1 to –1.

Consider two variables, X and Y. X is the independent variable, and Y is the dependent variable. A perfect correlation of +1 means that the value of Y increases by the same amount for each unit of increase in the value of X. A correlation of –1 indicates a perfect inverse relationship, in which the value of the dependent variable decreases by the same amount for each unit increase in the value of the independent variable. A correlation coefficient of zero indicates that no relationship exists between the dependent and independent variables. In other words, no consistent (that is, in one direction only) change in the value of the dependent variable occurs for each unit change in the value of the independent variable.

What do correlation coefficients mean? If you examine correlations graphically, you can see that the stronger the correlation (that is, the closer to +1 or to –1), the more it resembles a straight line. This is called a *linear relationship.*

Correlations are described graphically using scatterplots in which the numerical values of the two variables are expressed as points. Figure 3.1a shows a perfect negative correlation (–1) between two variables; Figure 3.1b, a perfect positive correlation (+1); and Figure 3.1c, no correlation at all. As you can see, the correlations of +1 and –1 look like a line. When a correlation is near zero, the shape of the pattern of observations is spread throughout and is somewhat circular. A correlation of .50 tends to be more oval.

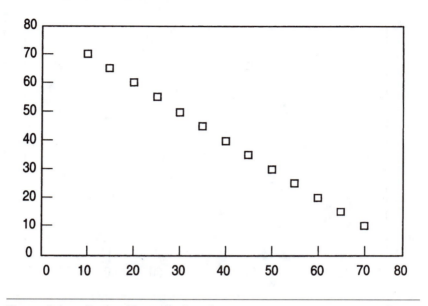

Figure 3.1a. Perfect Negative Correlation

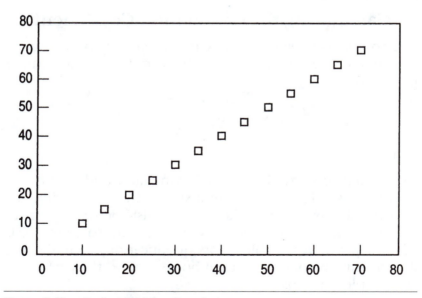

Figure 3.1b. Perfect Positive Correlation

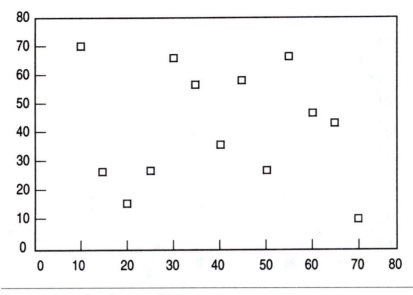

Figure 3.1c.   Correlation of Zero

Calculating the Correlation Coefficient

The correlation coefficient is symbolized as *r* and is usually reported to two decimal places. The formula for calculating *r* is as follows:

$$r = \frac{\Sigma(X - \overline{X})(Y - \overline{Y})}{\left(\sqrt{\Sigma(X - \overline{X})^2}\right)\left(\sqrt{\Sigma(Y - \overline{Y})^2}\right)}$$

The data displayed in the following table and used in the calculations below come from a survey that was conducted to determine whether a relationship exists between years of education and number of books read in the past year. *X* is the independent variable (years of education), and *Y* is the dependent variable (number of books read in the past year). Ten people participated in the survey.

Respondent	X	Y	$X - \bar{X}$ ($\bar{X} = 9.5$)	$Y - \bar{Y}$ ($\bar{Y} = 11.8$)	$(X - \bar{X})$ $(Y - \bar{Y})$	$(X - \bar{X})^2$	$(Y - \bar{Y})^2$
1	10	12	.5	.2	.1	.2	.04
2	12	14	2.5	2.2	5.5	6.2	4.8
3	5	7	−4.5	−4.8	21.6	20.2	23.0
4	7	9	−2.5	−2.8	7.0	6.2	7.8
5	7	10	−2.5	−1.8	4.5	6.2	3.2
6	12	15	2.5	3.2	8.0	6.2	10.2
7	10	13	.5	1.2	.6	.2	1.4
8	6	8	−3.5	−3.8	13.3	12.2	14.4
9	10	12	.5	.2	.1	.2	.04
10	16	18	6.5	6.2	40.3	42.3	38.4
Sum	95	118			101	100.1	103.3

1. Using the table to get each Σ in the formula, you see that

$$\Sigma(X - \bar{X})(Y - \bar{Y}) = 101$$
$$S(X - \bar{X})^2 (Y - \bar{Y})^2 = 101.1 \times 103$$

2. Filling in the formula, you get the following:

   a. $101 / \left(\sqrt{100.1}\right)\left(\sqrt{103.3}\right)$

   $\sqrt{100.1} = 10.0$ (rounded)

   $\sqrt{100.3} = 10.2$ (rounded)

   b. $101 / 10 \times 10.2 = .99$

   $10 \times 10.2 = 102$

   c. $101 / 102 = .99$

The correlation coefficient is .99, suggesting a nearly perfect relationship between years of education and number of books read in the past year.

A correlation coefficient measures only a straight-line, or linear, relationship. If the distribution of data for either the independent or the dependent variable is skewed or contains outlying values, you have a **curvilinear relationship.** In that case, you need to **transform the data** so that you can use conventional statistical methods (otherwise, you cannot). When you transform data, you change the scale of measurement. How will you know if the relationship is curvilinear? You should always plot the relationship. Use the computer to do this unless you have a relatively small sample and the time to plot the relationship by hand on graph paper.

Size of the Correlation

How Large Should a Correlation Be?
A Conservative Rule of Thumb

0 to +.25 (or −.25) = Little or no relationship

+.26 to +.50 (or −.26 to −.50) = Fair degree of
relationship

+.51 to +.75 = (or −.51 to −.75) = Moderate to good
relationship

Over +.75 (or −.75) = Very good to excellent relationship

For some social science disciplines, correlations of .26 to .50 are considered quite high, especially if they occur in multiple regression models where one variable is estimated by the use of more than one other variable.

The adequacy of a correlation is largely situational. For example, if the correlation between scores on your new and supposedly efficient attitude inventory and an older, supposedly more cumbersome one is .75, you might feel just fine until you find out that the correlation between someone else's inventory and the older one is .90.

Other than for values of +1, 0, and –1, however, correlation coefficients are not easy to interpret. We know, for example, that two variables with a correlation of .50 have a direct but imperfect relationship. Can we say that a correlation of .50 is half that of 1? Actually, to answer this question, you must make use of another statistic: the coefficient of determination, or r^2.

The r^2 tells the proportion of variation in the dependent variable that is associated with variation or changes in the independent variable. For a correlation coefficient of .50, the coefficient of determination is $.50^2$, or .25. This means that you can predict 25% of the variation in one measure (e.g., number of books read) by knowing the value of the other (e.g., years of education)—or the other way around. A correlation of .50 describes an association that is one-fourth as strong as a correlation of 1. In the example above (years of education and number of books read), where the correlation coefficient is .99, the coefficient of determination is .99 × .99, or 98%. In this case, 98% of the variation in number of books read can be predicted based on knowledge of the number of years of education—or the other way around.

WARNING

🚫 Use correlations to estimate the relationship between two characteristics. Do *not* use them to make claims regarding cause and effect, or causation. A correlation analysis can show that years of education and numbers of books read are strongly related, but it cannot confirm that people read many books because they have many years of education. For one thing, a preference for reading may be the cause of many years of education, or years of education and number of books read may be "caused" by a third factor—for example, a relatively high income.

Ordinal Data and Correlation

The **Spearman rank correlation** (also named after a statistician), sometimes called *Spearman's rho,* is often used to describe the relationship between two ordinal characteristics or one ordinal and one numerical characteristic, as in Example 3.1. Spearman's rho is also used with numerical data when the observations are skewed, with respondent outliers. In fact, if the median is the appropriate statistic to use in measuring central tendency, Spearman's rho is the correct correlation procedure.

The symbol for Spearman's rho is r_s. To calculate r_s, you need to begin by putting the data in "rank" order (e.g., from highest to lowest score). Spearman's rho ranges from +1 to –1, with +1 and –1 meaning perfect correlation between the ranks rather than the numerical values.

EXAMPLE 3.1
Using Spearman's Rho

To describe relationships between two ordinal characteristics:

- Does a relationship exist between ratings of satisfaction and ratings of preferences for leisure-time activities?

- Does a relationship exist between level of education and ratings of satisfaction?

To describe relationships between one ordinal and one numerical characteristic:

- Does a relationship exist between level of education and quantity of sports equipment purchased in the past year?

- Does a relationship exist between preference ratings and number of trips taken for pleasure?

Regression

One of the major differences between correlation analysis and **regression analysis** is that correlation describes a relationship whereas regression predicts a value. Regression analysis is concerned with estimating the components of a mathematical model that reflects the relationship between the dependent and independent variables in the population. To make the estimate, you assume that the relationship between variables is linear and that a straight line can be used to summarize the data. Regression is often referred to as *linear regression* or *simple linear regression*. There is, however, nothing simple about regression analysis. This discussion is intended to help you to understand its uses and interpret the results, but you will probably need more information than is presented here to conduct regression analysis or to debate with statisticians the virtues of the alternative regression methods.

A common method for fitting a line to the data or observations is called *least squares*. Suppose you interview a sample of teenage mothers to determine the extent to which County A's outreach program was responsible for encouraging them to keep their recommended number of prenatal care appointments. The regression equation would look like this:

Predicted number of visits = a + b (outreach).

This equation can be illustrated graphically as shown in Figure 3.2. In the figure, you see a Y-axis (vertical) and an X-axis (horizontal). The line crosses the Y-axis at a (this point is called the *intercept*). The slope of the line indicates the amount of change in Y for each unit change in X. If the slope is positive, Y increases as X increases; if the slope is negative, Y decreases as X increases. In the example above, in which

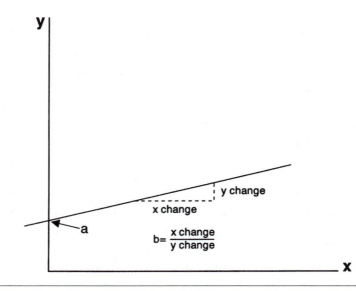

Figure 3.2.   Graphic Interpretation of Regression Line

your interest is the ability to relate prenatal care visits and the county's outreach teen program, *a* is the predicted number of visits without outreach. The slope, *b,* is the change in predicted number of visits for a unit of change in outreach. Stated another way, *b* is the amount of change in number of visits per outreach activity.

In regression, the slope in the population is symbolized by β_1 (Greek letter beta with a subscript 1), called the regression coefficient; β_0 denotes the intercept of the regression line. Also, the values of the *Y*s provided from the regression equation are predicted rather than actual values. The symbol Y, is used to distinguish predicted values from actual values. Because not all predictions are perfect, the regression model contains an error term, *e.* This is the amount the actual values of *Y* depart from the predicted values based on the regression line. The formula for the regression model is as follows:

$$Y, = \beta_0 + \beta_1 X + e$$

A Note on the Relationship Between Two Nominal Characteristics

Survey researchers are usually interested in the significance of the relationship between two nominal variables rather than in just the relationship itself. For example, you are more likely to be concerned with determining whether the number of women answering yes to a particular question is statistically different from the number of men answering yes than you are in the extent of agreement between the numbers of women and men answering yes. Among the techniques available for determining the significance of the differences between nominal variables are chi-square and Fisher's exact test. The chi-square distribution is described in Chapter 4. To use it appropriately, you first need to understand the normal distribution and hypothesis testing.

The Normal Distribution

The **normal distribution** is a smooth, bell-shaped curve that is continuous and symmetric around the mean; it is symbolized by μ (Greek letter mu). The standard deviation is symbolized by σ (Greek lowercase letter sigma). The mean ±1 standard deviation contains approximately 68% of the area under the normal curve, the mean ±2 standard deviations contain approximately 95% of the area under the normal curve, and the mean ±3 standard deviations contain approximately 99% of the area under the normal curve.

A normally distributed random variable with a mean and standard deviation can be transformed to a standard normal, or *z* distribution. This distribution has a mean of 0 and a standard deviation of 1. The *z* transformation expresses the deviation from the mean in standard deviation units. You can transform any normal distribution to the *z* distribution by using this formula:

$$z = X - \beta / \sigma$$

But what is a normal distribution of survey data or observations, and how do you know if you have one? When you study the population at large, certain variables (such as height, weight, and blood pressure) are considered normally distributed, that is, with 99% of the observations falling within ±3 standard deviations of the mean. In actuality, perfectly normal distributions are as rare as perfectly normal people (this is true even for the distribution of height, weight, and blood pressure). Some distributions, however, are more normal than others.

There are many computer programs available that will tell you graphically if a distribution is normal. If you prefer, you can plot the data yourself in the form of a histogram or box-and-whisker plot. A histogram uses area to describe the frequency distribution of numerical observations.

If a distribution is normal, you can use statistical methods that assume normality, such as the *t* test. If a distribution is not normal, you must transform the data to make them normal or use statistical methods that are not dependent on normal distributions.

Comparisons: Hypothesis Testing, *p* Values, and Confidence Levels

Survey studies often compare two or more groups, such as men and women, experimental and control participants, Team A and Team B, or students in the United States and students elsewhere. If differences exist, survey researchers analyze the magnitude of the differences for significance. When you are comparing one nominal independent variable (e.g., experimental and control group) with respect to one numerical dependent variable (e.g., attitudes as measured by a score), you can use a two-sample, independent groups *t* test. The use of this statistical test, one of the most common, is illustrated in Example 3.2.

EXAMPLE 3.2
Comparing Two Groups: The *t* Test

Situation

Employees of the school district have always run the schools' cafeterias. In recent years, the quality and efficiency of the cafeterias have diminished. An outside consulting group is called in to recommend ways to improve the management of the cafeterias. The consultants suggest that having a private company, rather than the district, manage the cafeterias may be the answer. School district officials agree. After a bidding process,

Example 3.2 continued

the district awards a contract to the Great Food Company to manage several school cafeterias. After 2 years, students, teachers, administrators, and other personnel at several schools (some where the cafeterias are managed by Great Food and some where they are managed by the district) are surveyed regarding their opinions of the quality of the food and the service and efficiency of the cafeterias at their schools.

Expectations

A statistically significant difference in opinions will be found favoring Great Food over the district. The survey team will assess opinions using the results of a 100-point survey.

Analysis

The survey team will apply a *t* test in comparing the opinions of the two groups (schools where the cafeterias are managed by Great Food and schools where they are managed by the district) regarding the quality and efficiency of food service.

In the example, a survey is conducted after 2 years to find out if an experimental protocol involving a private company has improved the quality and efficiency of the cafeterias in selected schools. A survey is conducted with teachers, students, administrators, and others at participating and nonparticipating schools, and the results are compared. The survey has 100 points; a 15-point difference is needed in favor of the private company for the experiment to be considered a success.

Example 3.2 mentions a "statistically significant difference." *Statistical significance* is a very important concept. To be statistically significant, differences must be attributable to a planned intervention (e.g., Great Food's new management efforts) rather than to chance or historical occurrences (e.g., a change in expectations regarding the cafeteria that comes about because most students eat somewhere else).

Statistical significance is often interpreted to mean a result that happens by chance less than once in 20 times, with a **p value** (that is, the probability of obtaining the results by chance) less than or equal to .05. The **null hypothesis** states that no difference exists in the means (scores or other numerical values) obtained by two groups. Statistical significance occurs when the null hypothesis is rejected (suggesting that a difference does exist).

The following section provides a more detailed explanation of these terms and a guide for conducting a hypothesis test and determining statistical significance.

Guide to Hypothesis Testing, Statistical Significance, and *p* Values

1. *State the null hypothesis.* The null hypothesis (H_0) is a statement that no difference exists between the averages or means of two groups. The following are typical null hypotheses:

-   No difference exists between the means of the experimental program and the control program. (For example, no difference exists between privately and publicly managed school cafeterias.)

-   No difference exists between the sample's (the survey's participants) mean and the mean of the population from which the participants were sampled. (For example, no difference exists between the sample of teachers chosen to be interviewed and those who were not chosen.)

The **alternative or research hypothesis**, H_1, is a statement that disagrees with the null hypothesis:

A difference exists between the means of the experimental program and the control program. (For example, a difference exists between privately and publicly managed school cafeterias.)

A difference exists between the sample's (the survey's participants) mean and the mean of the population from which the participants were sampled. (For example, differences exist between the sample of teachers chosen to be interviewed and those who were not chosen.)

When no difference in means is found, the result is termed a *failure to reject the null hypothesis*. Note that this is not the same as "acceptance of the null hypothesis," and you should avoid stating it as such. Conceptualizing a finding of no difference in means as a failure to reject the null suggests that a difference probably does *not* exist between the means—say, between the mean opinion scores in School A and those in School B. If the null is rejected, then a difference exists between the mean opinion scores, in favor of the alternative or research hypothesis.

When you have no reason to suspect in advance which of two scores is better, you use a **two-tailed hypothesis test.** When you have an alternative hypothesis in mind—say, A is better than B—you use a **one-tailed test**. The "tails" in hypothesis testing are the extreme ends of a statistical distribution. The idea is that if you obtain a statistic that is way out in one or the other of the tails, or at the end of the expected distribution (according to or derived from the null hypothesis distribution), then you reject the null.

2.   *State the level of significance for the statistical test (e.g., the* t *test)* being used. The level of significance, when chosen before the test is performed, is called the alpha value (denoted by the Greek letter α). The **alpha** is the probability of rejecting the null hypothesis when it is actually true. Tradition keeps the alpha value small— .05, .01, or .001—because you do not want to reject a null hypothesis when in fact it is true and there is no difference between group means.

The *p* value is the probability that a difference at least as large as the obtained difference would have come about if the means were really equal. The *p,* which is calculated *after* the statistical test, is sometimes called the *observed* or *obtained significance level.* If the *p* value, or observed significance, is less than alpha, then the null is rejected.

Current practice requires the specification of exact or obtained *p* values. That is, if the obtained *p* is .03, you should report that number rather than *p* < .05. Reporting the approximate *p* was common practice when researchers had to use tables in statistics texts to find the critical values of a distribution. The critical value is the absolute value that a test statistic must exceed for the null hypothesis to be rejected.

Although all statistical software programs give exact *p*s, the practice of reporting approximations (<.05, <.01, <.001) has not been eradicated. The merit of using exact values is that, without them, a finding of *p* = .06 may be viewed as not significant, whereas a finding of *p* = .05 will be.

3.   *Determine the critical value the test statistic must attain to be significant.* Each test statistic, such as the mean, *t, F,* and chi-square, has a distribution. This is called the **sampling distribution.** Its mean is called the **expected value,** and its variability is called the **standard error.**

Every test statistic distribution is divided into an area of rejection and an area of acceptance. With a one-tailed test, the rejection area is *either* the upper or the lower end or tail of the distribution. With a two-tailed test, there are two areas of rejection: one in each tail of the distribution.

You can find critical values in statistical tables, which are available in most statistics textbooks. For example, for the z distribution with an alpha of .05 and a two-tailed test, tabular values will show that the area of acceptance for the null hypothesis is the central 95% of the z distribution and that the areas of rejection are the 2.5% in each tail. The value of z that defines these areas is –1.96 for the lower tail and +1.96 for the upper tail. If the test statistic is less than –1.96 or greater than +1.96, it will be rejected. The areas of acceptance and rejection in a standard normal distribution, using $\alpha = .05$, are illustrated in Figure 3.3.

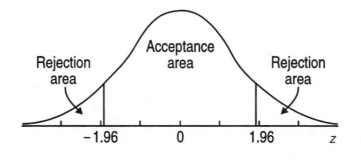

Figure 3.3.   Areas of Acceptance and Rejection in a Standard Normal Distribution, Using ? = .05

4.   *Perform the calculation.* To make statistical computations, you can use one of the numerous statistical software packages that are available. To choose the best software for your needs, you might need to do a little

research. You can find out about the features of different programs by reading the software reviews in professional journals of education, business, law, statistics, epidemiology, and medicine. You might also ask colleagues for their recommendations. All statistical packages have manuals (and/or tutorials) that will teach you how to create data files and give the appropriate commands.

Risk and Odds

Statements of risk and odds are alternative ways of describing the likelihood that particular outcomes will occur. Suppose you are conducting a survey to find out about people's sleeping problems. You find that of every 100 people who have trouble sleeping, 20 report frequent problems. You can state that among those who have trouble sleeping, the *risk* of having frequent problems is 20/100 or 0.20. The *odds* of someone having frequent problems with sleeping are calculated differently. To get the odds, you subtract the number of persons with frequent problems (20) from the total (100) and use the result (80) as the denominator. Thus, the odds that someone who has trouble sleeping is having frequent sleeping problems are 20/80 or 0.25. The different ways in which risk and odds are calculated are compared in Example 3.3.

EXAMPLE 3.3

The Calculation of Risk and Odds

Number of Persons With Outcome	Risk	Odds
20 of 100	20/100 = 0.20	20/80 = 0.25
40 of 100	40/100 = 0.40	40/80 = 0.66
50 of 100	50/100 = 0.50	50/80 = 1.00
90 of 100	90/100 = 0.90	90/80 = 9.00

Because statements of risk and odds are really just different ways of expressing the same relationship, risk can be derived from odds, and vice versa. You can convert risk to odds by dividing it by 1 minus the risk, and you can convert odds to risk by dividing odds by 1 plus the odds.

$$Odds = (Risk)/(1 - Risk)$$

$$Risk = (Odds)/(1 + Odds)$$

When an outcome is infrequent, little difference exists in the numerical values between odds and risk. When the outcome is frequent, however, differences emerge. If, for instance, 20 of 100 persons with sleeping problems have frequent sleeping problems, the risk and odds are similar: 0.20 and 0.25, respectively. If 90 of those 100 persons have frequent problems, then the risk is 0.90 and the odds are 9.00.

ODDS RATIOS AND RELATIVE RISK

Odds ratios are often useful for comparing nominal dependent variables between groups. They allow you to give an estimate of the strength of the relationship between the variables. For example, suppose you have evidence that people with sleeping problems take naps in the afternoons. You want to check out the strength of the relationship between afternoon naps and subsequent nightly sleeping problems. You put together two groups: people with sleeping problems and people without. You ask each person in both groups, "Do you take naps in the afternoon?" Their response choices are yes or no.

To analyze the responses, you might create a 2 x 2 table such as the following:

Sleeping Problems

Nap in Afternoon	Yes	No
Yes	A	B
No	C	D

You would create a 2 x 2 table because you have two variables with two levels: nap (yes or no) and sleeping problems (yes or no). Notice that there are 4 cells in the table for data entry. The two variables, nap in the afternoon and sleeping problems, are nominal variables.

If you were interested only in whether there are statistical differences in the numbers of people in each of the cells, you could use the chi-square test, but that will not tell you about the strength of the relationship between the variables. A chi-square test will only allow you to infer differences. An odds ratio, in contrast, will allow you to say something like this: The odds of having sleeping problems are greater (or less) among people who nap (or do not nap) in the afternoon.

The odds ratio is used in case-control studies. In such a study, the researcher decides how many "cases" (e.g., people who have sleeping problems) and "controls" (e.g., people who do not have sleeping problems) to include. (For more about case-control designs, see **How to Design Survey Studies,** Volume 6 in this series.) To calculate the odds ratio, the researcher counts the number in each group who have the "risk factor" (e.g., napping during the day) and divides the odds of having the risk factor among the cases by the odds of having the risk factor among the controls.

The vocabulary associated with the use of odds ratios—including terms such as *case control* and *risk factor*—comes from the study of public health problems, but odds ratios are now used widely in many fields. They are also integral components of other statistical methods. If you do logistic regressions or have to interpret them, your analytic program will automatically yield odds ratios.

Example 3.4 shows the formula for the odds ratio, and Example 3.5 gives an example of how the formula works.

EXAMPLE 3.4

The Formula for the Odds Ratio

Risk Factor Present?	Case	Control	Total
Yes	a	b	a + b
No	c	d	c + d
Total	a + c	b + d	n

EXAMPLE 3.5
Using the Odds Ratio

Suppose you are interested in the relationship between napping in the afternoon (the risk factor) and sleeping problems. You ask the question: When compared with people who do not take afternoon naps, what is the likelihood that people who do will have sleeping problems?

You identify 400 people with sleeping problems and 400 without, and you find that among all people with problems, 100 take naps and 300 do not. Among people without sleeping problems, 50 take naps. To compare the odds of sleeping problems between the two groups, you put the data into a 2 × 2 table:

Example 3.5 continued

Sleeping Problems

Nap in Afternoon	Case	Control	Total
Yes	100	50	150
No	300	400	700
Total	400	400	800

Using the data in Example 3.5, you can calculate the odds ratio (OR) as follows:

$$OR = ad/bc = 100 \times 400/50 \times 300 = 40,000/15,000 = 2.67.$$

The odds of being exposed to the risk factor (nap in the afternoon) are thus 2.67 higher for people in the sample with sleeping problems than for people without sleeping problems. The answer to the question is that people is who take afternoon naps are 2.67 times more likely to encounter sleeping problems than people who do not take afternoon naps.

Risk ratios are also used to examine the strength of the relationship between two nominal variables, but the design for studying the relationship is quite different. It is a cohort design. (For more on cohort designs, see **How to Design Survey Studies**, Volume 6 in this series.) Suppose you want to determine the likelihood that people who nap during the day have nightly sleeping problems. First you pick the cohort, which, in this situation, is people with sleeping problems. Then you select a period of time to observe them, say, 12 months. At the end of the 12 months, you count the number of people in the cohort who had sleeping problems and the number of people who did not. You are interested in finding out whether they differ and, if so, whether a greater risk was likely for people who napped.

When you rely on cohort designs in calculating risk ratios (also called *relative risks* or *likelihood ratios*), you have no control over how many people are in each group. Obviously, you cannot control the numbers of people in the study group who develop sleeping problems, although you do have control over the number of people in your study group. The surveyor who uses a case-control design has control over the number of people who have and do not have the problem of interest. He or she can say: I will have 100 cases and 100 controls. It may take the case-control surveyor more or less than 12 months to identify enough cases for each group. In technical terms, the risk ratio is the ratio of the incidence of "disease" (e.g., sleeping problems) among the "exposed" (people who nap) to the incidence of "disease" among the "nonexposed" (people who do not nap). Incidence rates can be estimated only prospectively.

In a case-control study, you cannot estimate the probability of having a problem because you have determined in advance how many people are in the cases and how many are in the controls. All you can do is determine the probability of having the risk factor. This is unusual; normally, researchers are concerned with finding out the probability of having the problem, not the risk for the problem. However, when you compare odds in an odds ratio, you will find that the ratio of the odds for having the risk factor is identical to the ratio of the odds for having the disease or problem. Thus, you can calculate the same odds ratio for a case-control study as for a cohort study or randomized, controlled trial. It doesn't matter which variable is the independent and which is the dependent—the odds ratio will have exactly the same value. This is not true of risk ratios, and so researchers find odds ratios to be an excellent way to answer questions or test hypotheses involving nominal dependent variables between groups defined by nominal independent variables.

4

Selecting Commonly Used Statistical Methods for Surveys

$\mathbf{T}$his chapter discusses the data-analytic methods that are most commonly used in survey studies and provides some guidance for choosing among them. Table 4.1 is a general guide to the methods available and their typical uses. For the sake of simplicity, the table omits ordinal variables. When independent variables are measured on an ordinal scale, they are often treated as if they were nominal. For example, to predict the outcomes of participation in a program for clients with good, fair, and poor emotional health, rather than treating good, fair, and poor as ordinal variables, you can convert them to nominal variables: good, yes or no; fair, yes or no; poor, yes or no.

When dependent variables are measured on an ordinal scale, they are habitually treated as if they were numerical.

TABLE 4.1   General Guide to the Selection of Data-Analytic Methods for Surveys

Sample Survey Objective	Type of Data		Potential Analytic Method
	Independent Variable	Dependent Variable	
For objectives with one independent and one dependent variable			
To compare experimental and control counties in children's reported use of or failure to use bicycle helmets	Nominal: group (experimental and control)	Nominal: use of helmets (used helmets or did not)	Chi-square; Fisher's exact test
To compare experimental and control groups in their attitudes (measured by their scores on the Attitude Survey)	Nominal (dichotomous): group (experimental and control)	Numerical (attitude scores)	One-sample *t* test, dependent *t* test, and independent samples *t* test; Wilcoxon signed-ranks test; Wilcoxon rank-sum test (the Mann-Whitney *U*)
To compare teens in the United States, Canada, and England with respect to their attitudes (measured by their scores on the Attitude Survey)	Nominal (more than two values): United States, Canada, and England	Numerical (attitude scores)	One-way analysis of variance (uses the *F* test)
To determine whether high scores on the Attitude Survey predict high scores on the Knowledge Test	Numerical (attitude scores)	Numerical (knowledge scores)	Regression (when neither variable is independent or dependent, use correlation)

TABLE 4.1 Continued

Sample Survey Objective	Type of Data		Potential Analytic Method
	Independent Variable	Dependent Variable	
For objectives with two or more independent variables			
To compare men and women in the experimental and control programs in terms of whether or not they adhered to a diet	Nominal (gender, group)	Nominal (adhered or did not adhere to a diet	Log-linear
To compare men and women with differing scores on the Knowledge Test in terms of whether or not they adhered to a diet	Nominal (gender) and numerical (knowledge scores)	Nominal and dichotomous (adhered or did not adhere to a diet)	Logistic regression
To compare men and women in the experimental and control programs with respect to their attitudes (measured by their scores on the Attitude Survey)	Nominal (gender and group)	Numerical (attitude scores)	Analysis of variance (ANOVA)
To determine whether age, income, and years living in the community are related to attitudes (measured by scores on the Attitude Survey)	Numerical (age, income, and years living in the community)	Numerical (attitude scores)	Multiple regression

TABLE 4.1   Continued

| Sample Survey Objective | Type of Data | | Potential Analytic Method |
	Independent Variable	Dependent Variable	
To compare men and women in the experimental and control programs in their attitudes (measured by their scores on the Attitude Survey) when their level of education is controlled	Nominal (gender and group) with confounding factors (such as education)	Numerical (attitude scores)	Analysis of covariance (ANCOVA)
For objectives with two or more independent and dependent variables			
To compare men and women in the experimental and control programs in their attitude and knowledge scores	Nominal (gender and group)	Numerical (scores on two measures: attitudes and knowledge)	Multivariate analysis of variance (MANOVA)

Suppose the dependent variable in a nutrition program is men's and women's ratings of self-esteem (10 = *very high* and 1 = *very low*). The dependent ordinal variable can, for the sake of the analysis, be regarded as numerical, and mean ratings can be computed.

Before you conduct any statistical analysis, you should check the assumptions of the analysis method in a statistics text or computer manual. If the survey data do not meet the assumptions, you will need to look for other statistical methods to use. Even if your data appear to meet the assumptions, you should check once again after you perform the analysis. If you are using correlations or regressions, do the data meet the assumptions concerning linearity? If you are using an independent *t* test, are the variances equal?

The **chi-square**, *t* **test**, and **analysis of variance (ANOVA)** are introduced later in this chapter because of their utility in analyzing survey data. Table 4.1 also mentions some methods for analyzing data that are not discussed in this book. These complex methods build upon the principles and assumptions included in this overview. For further information about these methods, see the sources listed in the "Suggested Readings" section at the end of this book.

Reading Computer Output

Suppose you do a chi-square analysis. The computer output will contain the results of the analysis itself as well as additional information; how these elements are presented, and what is included in them (e.g., what additional tests and data), will vary depending on the statistical program used. As a survey researcher, you need to become multilingual in output terms so that you can adequately read and talk about a range of statistical programs. Experience with various programs helps; the following subsections introduce you to two commonly used statistical techniques and their corresponding outputs in one program application.

CHI-SQUARE

The chi-square (represented by the Greek letter chi with a superscript 2: χ^2) distribution is the most commonly used method of comparing proportions. Suppose you survey 208 high school seniors to find out their career preferences. Of this group, 103 have spent a year in a special job-training program; the others have not. The survey finds that 40 seniors prefer to go on to college before seeking employment, whereas the remainder prefer to enter the labor force immediately.

The questions you are interested in answering are these:

1. Does a difference exist between program participants and the others in the number or proportion of seniors preferring to continue their education?

2. Does an association (or relationship) exist between being in the program and also preferring to continue in college?

To answer these questions, you could create a table that looks like this:

	Marginal Frequencies		
	Job Program	No Program	Total
Prefer college			40
Do not prefer college			168
Total	103	105	208

The marginal frequencies represent the numbers or proportions of seniors in the two survey groups. The expected frequencies shown in the following table represent the numbers or proportions of seniors in each cell, assuming that no relationship (the null hypothesis) exists between preference and program participation:

	Expected Frequencies		
	Job Program	No Program	Total
Prefer college	20	20	40
Do not prefer college	84	84	168
Total	104	104	208

The expected frequencies are the hypothetical distribution if the views of the two groups being compared are alike. So if 40 people prefer college, as the illustrative survey finds, then the expected frequencies are 20 in the job program group and 20 in the group of nonparticipants.

Chi-square tests enable you to compare the expected frequency in each cell with the frequency that actually occurs (the observed frequency). The observed frequencies are the survey's data. The differences between observed and expected frequencies are combined to form the chi-square statistic. If a relationship exists between the column and row variables in a table such as the one above (e.g., whether or not the person is in a program and his or her preference), the two are said to be *dependent*. In this case, you would decide in favor of differences between the groups.

The following notation will assist you in using chi-square tests with two groups (e.g., experimental and control) and a two-pronged dichotomous nominal survey outcome (e.g., yes, prefer college, or no, do not prefer college):

	Experimental	Control	Total
Positive	a	b	a + b
Negative	c	d	c + d
Total	a + c	b + d	a + b + c + d = n

This is called a 2 x 2 table. The formula for calculating the chi-square for data in a 2 x 2 table is as follows:

$$\chi^2(1) = n(ad - bc)^2 / (a + c)(b + d)(a + b)(c + d)$$

The (1) in the equation refers to the degrees of freedom, a parameter that is used also in the t distribution. A parameter is the population (as contrasted with a sample) value of a distribution (e.g., the mean of the population is μ, and the standard deviation is σ). The chi-square test is performed as a one-tailed test. If the observed frequencies depart from the expected frequencies by more than the amount that you can expect by chance, you reject the null.

Going back to the example of preferences for college in a comparison of program and nonprogram participants, suppose the 2 x 2 table is filled out to look like this:

	Jobs Program	No Program	Total
Prefer college	80	30	110
Do not prefer college	23	75	98
Total	103	105	208

Using the formula above, you would have the following calculations:

$$\chi^2(1) = n(ad - bc)^2 / (a + c)(b + d)(a + b)(c + d)$$

$$\chi^2 = \frac{208[(80)(75) - (30)(23)]^2}{(103)(105)(110)(98)}$$

$$\chi^2 = \frac{208(5310)^2}{116585700}$$

$$\chi^2 = 50.30$$

The critical value for an α of .01 is 6.635. In other words, 99% of the distribution is below 6.635. (You cannot possibly memorize all critical values, but with experience you will become familiar with many.) Any obtained value above the critical value enables you to reject the null hypothesis that no difference exists between the program and no-program groups. In the example, the obtained statistic is above the critical value, and so the null is rejected. The conclusion is that differences exist between the groups and preference for college is related to program participation.

Chi-square tests can be performed with many numbers of columns and rows. Sometimes, researchers "correct" chi-square values with a continuity correction or Yates's correction. The correction involves subtracting 0.5 from the absolute value of (ad − bc) before squaring. Its purpose is to lower the value of the obtained statistic, reducing the risk of a Type I error (rejecting the null when it is true); however, the risk of a Type II error (failing to reject the null when it is false) increases. Finally, when the expected frequencies are small (less than 5), Fisher's exact test can be used (for more about this method, consult the appropriate sources in the "Suggested Readings" section at the end of this book).

Example 4.1 illustrates how to read chi-square output from one sample program (SPSS/PC+). As you can see, along with the significance of the differences, a number of other statistics are also provided. The particular statistics that appear in computer output vary in importance according to the complexity of the survey and the computer program you use.

EXAMPLE 4.1
Reading Computer Output: Chi-Square

Concern has been raised that unemployed people in Community A do not have adequate access to health care; because of this, they do not get to see physicians when they need to. Does a difference exist in the use of health care services between people who are employed and those who are unemployed? More specifically, does the proportion of people who have paying jobs differ from the proportion who do not in terms of whether or not they have seen any doctor (MD) more than once?

Type of Survey: Self-administered questionnaire

Survey Questions:

- In the past year, did you see any MD more than once? (yes or no)

- In the past year, did you have a full- or part-time paying job that lasted 9 months or more? (yes or no)

Independent Variable: Job status (having a full- or part-time paying job or not having one)

Dependent Variable: Use of health services (seeing an MD more than once)

Analysis Method: Chi-square

Computer Output: (sample)

Example 4.1 continued

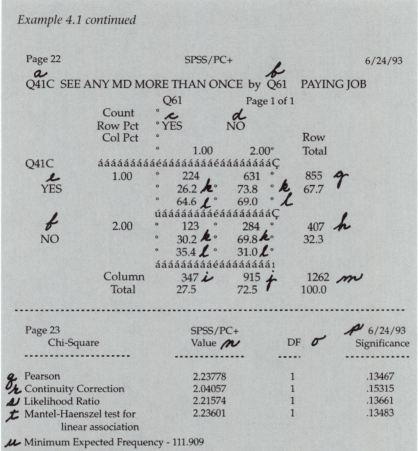

Page 22   SPSS/PC+   6/24/93

a

Q41C SEE ANY MD MORE THAN ONCE by *b* Q61   PAYING JOB

		Q61		Page 1 of 1
	Count	*c*	*d*	
	Row Pct	YES	NO	
	Col Pct			Row
		1.00	2.00	Total
Q41C				
e YES	1.00	224	631	855 *g*
		26.2 *k*	73.8 *k*	67.7
		64.6 *l*	69.0 *l*	
f NO	2.00	123	284	407 *h*
		30.2 *k*	69.8 *k*	32.3
		35.4 *l*	31.0 *l*	
	Column	347 *i*	915 *j*	1262 *m*
	Total	27.5	72.5	100.0

Page 23	SPSS/PC+		*p* 6/24/93
Chi-Square	Value *n*	DF *o*	Significance
q Pearson	2.23778	1	.13467
r Continuity Correction	2.04057	1	.15315
s Likelihood Ratio	2.21574	1	.13661
t Mantel-Haenszel test for linear association	2.23601	1	.13483

u Minimum Expected Frequency - 111.909

Number of Missing Observations: 20

Interpretation: (refer to corresponding letters marked on the computer output)

  a. Q41c refers to the question on the self-administered questionnaire that asks whether the respondent has seen any MD more than once.

Example 4.1 continued

b. Q61 refers to the question on the self-administered questionnaire that asks whether the respondent has a paying job.

c. Yes is the column that refers to the positive answer to the question about having a paying job.

d. No is the column that refers to the negative answer to the question about having a paying job.

e. Yes is the row that pertains to the positive answer to the question about seeing or not seeing any MD.

f. No is the row that pertains to the negative answer to the question about seeing or not seeing any MD.

g. Total number (855) and percentage (67.7) of people who saw an MD more than once.

h. Total number (407) and percentage (32.3) of people who did not see an MD more than once.

i. Total number (347) and percentage (27.5) of people who have a paying job.

j. Total number (915) and percentage (72.5) of people who do not have a paying job.

Example 4.1 continued

k. and l. Percentage of people represented in each cell. For example, in the top left-hand cell (Cell a), there are 224 respondents. They represent 26.2% of the 855 who saw any MD more than once and 64.6% of the 347 who also have a paying job.

m. Total number of respondents (1,262).

n. Value refers to the results of the statistical computation.

o. Degrees of freedom.

p. Obtained *p* value. This value is compared to alpha. If it is less, the null is rejected.

q. Pearson is the particular type of chi-square statistic calculated by this particular statistical package.

r. Continuity correction involves subtracting 0.5 from the difference between observed and expected frequencies before squaring to make the chi-square value smaller.

s. The likelihood ratio is the odds that the results occur in respondents who have seen any MD more than once versus those who have not.

t. Mantel-Haenszel test for linear association is a log-rank test for comparing two survival distributions. Computer programs routinely produce a variety of statistical tests. Each

Example 4.1 continued

contributes to an understanding of the main test results. (Unless you are planning to learn statistics, it is wise to check out the meaning of each statistical test on the output. Ask a statistician for advice or consult the sources listed in the "Suggested Readings" section at the end of this book.)

u. Minimum expected frequency will tell you if you have enough observations to proceed with the chi-square test or if you should consider Fisher's exact test.

Conclusion: The obtained significance level is .13467. The null hypothesis (no differences exist between respondents with and without paying jobs in whether or not they saw any MD) is retained. Put another way, we do not have enough evidence to reject the null hypothesis.

t TEST

The *t* test's probability distribution is similar to the standard normal distribution, or *z*. The *t* test is used to test hypotheses about means and thus requires numerical data. The shape of a *t* distribution approaches the bell shape of a standard normal distribution, which also has a mean of 0 and a standard deviation of 1, as the sample size and degrees of freedom increase. In fact, when the sample has 30 or more respondents, the two curves are very similar, and you can use either distribution to answer statistical questions. Current practice in most fields, however, relies on the *t* distribution even with large samples. Three situations can arise in which *t* tests are appropriate, as illustrated in Example 4.2.

EXAMPLE 4.2
Three Situations and the *t* Test

Survey 1: Children's Birthday Gifts

Children who are students at McCarthy Elementary School receive an average of 4.2 birthday gifts each. How does this compare to the results obtained in a national survey on children and birthday gifts?

Type of t: One-sample *t*

Comment: The mean of a group is compared to a norm, or standard value (the results of the national survey).

Survey 2: Low-Fat Diet for Men at the Frozen Food Plant

Do average scores on the Feel Good Inventory change for 50 men at the local frozen food plant after they participate in the Low-Fat Diet Program?

Type of t: Dependent *t*

Comment: The means of a single group are compared at two times (before and after participation in the Low-Fat Diet Program).

Survey 3: Learning the Ballet

On average, how do men and women compare in their attitudes toward ballet after participation in a ballet exercise program? The highest possible score is 50 points.

Type of t: Independent *t*

Comment: The means of two independent groups are compared.

To apply the *t* test appropriately, you must be working with survey data that meet certain assumptions. To use the *t* distribution for one mean (as in Survey 1 in Example 4.2), the assumption is that the observations (e.g., scores) are normally distributed. Some computer programs provide probability plots that enable you to certify that the data are consistent with this assumption. Sometimes, you can examine the distribution yourself. If the data are not normally distributed, you can transform them into a normal distribution. Alternatively, you can decide not to use the *t* and instead use different statistical measures, called *nonparametric procedures,* to analyze the data. Nonparametric methods make no assumptions about the distribution of observed values.

To detect the difference between the means obtained by the same group, usually measured twice (as in Survey 2 in Example 4.2), you would use a paired design. With the paired *t,* the assumption is that the observations are distributed normally. If the survey data violate the assumption, you can use the Wilcoxon signed-ranks test, a commonly used nonparametric test for the difference between two paired samples. This method tests the hypothesis that the medians, rather than the means, are equal (see the sources listed in the "Suggested Readings" section for more information on this test).

The *t* test for independent groups (as in Survey 3 in Example 4.2) assumes that the observations are normally distributed and that the variances of the observations are equal. If the sample sizes are equal, unequal variances will not have a major effect on the significance level of the test. If they are not, you need to make a downward adjustment of the degrees of freedom (i.e., so that there are fewer degrees of freedom) and use separate variance estimates instead of the combined or "pooled" variance. The statistical test to compare variances is the *F* test; many computer programs that perform the *t* test also perform this test. If one of the assumptions of the independent *t* test is violated, an alternative is the nonparametric Wilcoxon rank-sum test (Mann-Whitney *U*). This test assesses the equality of medians rather than means, as does the Wilcoxon signed-ranks test. Example 4.3 provides a sample computer printout for a *t* test from SPSS-PC+.

EXAMPLE 4.3
Reading Computer Output:
Independent Samples *t* Test

County A's health planners are concerned that sicker people may not be using the People's Ambulatory Care (PACE) clinic as often as they should. A survey is conducted to find out if this concern warrants attention.

Type of Survey: Self-administered questionnaire

Survey Questions:

- In the past year, did you see any MD more than once? (yes or no)

- The 20 questions on the Instrumental Activities of Daily Living (IADL) measure concerning a person's ability to function and perform various tasks, including personal care and home chores. A score of 100 represents maximum functioning.

Independent Variable: Use of health services (seeing an MD more than once at PACE or not)

Dependent Variable: Ability to function (score on the IADL)

Analysis Method: t test

Computer Output: (sample)

Example 4.3 continued

Page 97   SPSS/PC+   6/23/93

Independent samples of   Q41D   -   SEE MD AT PACE CLINIC > 1 TIME

Group 1:   Q41   EQ   *a* 1.00   Group 2:   Q41   EQ   *b* 2.00

t-test for: IADL

	c Number of Cases	*d* Mean	*e* Standard Deviation	*f* Standard Error
Group 1	561	75.5246	23.957	1.011
Group 2	311	77.4358	24.112	1.367

	Pooled *i* Variance Estimate			Separate *j* Variance Estimate		
g F Value	*h* 2-Tail Prob.	t Value	Degrees of Freedom	2-Tail Prob.	t Value	Degrees of Freedom	2-Tail Prob.
1.01	.890	–1.13	870	.261	–1.12	636.61	.262

Interpretation: (refer to corresponding letters marked on the computer output)

a. Group 1 answered yes to the question "Did you see an MD at the PACE clinic more than once this year?" The choices were 1 = yes and 2 = no.

b. Group 2 answered no to the question "Did you see an MD at the PACE clinic more than once this year?"

c. Number of cases refers to the number of respondents (sample size) in each group.

d. Mean score obtained on the IADL by each group.

Example 4.3 continued

e. Standard deviation of the scores.

f. Standard error of the means.

g. *F* value or statistic obtained in the test to determine the equality of the variances.

h. Probability of obtaining a result like the *F* value if the null is true. If the obtained probability is less than some agreed-on alpha such as .05 or .01, the null is rejected. In this case, the probability of .890 is greater than .05, and so the null is retained. The conclusion is that no differences exist in the variances of the two groups.

i. The pooled variance estimate is used when variances are equal. The *p* value is .261, greater than an alpha of .05. The null hypothesis regarding the equality of the group means is retained.

j. The separate variance estimate is used when variances are not equal.

Conclusion: No differences exist in functioning between respondents who saw a doctor at the PACE clinic more than one time and those who did not.

ANALYSIS OF VARIANCE (ANOVA)

Analysis of variance (commonly abbreviated as ANOVA) is used to compare the means of three or more groups. For instance, if you want to compare the mean achievement test scores in reading and math of children in Korea, Japan, and Singapore, you would use ANOVA. With ANOVA you ask the question, Does an *overall* difference exist among the groups? If the results are significant, you can then ask, Which combinations or pairs are responsible for the difference?

ANOVA guards against multiple Type I errors. (As noted above, a Type I error occurs when you reject the null although in fact no difference exists.) If you were to use *t* tests and an alpha of .05 to compare mean reading scores among children from Singapore, Korea, and Japan, you would need to conduct three separate tests: Singapore and Korea, Singapore and Japan, and Japan and Korea. With three tests, you have a 15% (3 × 5%) chance of incorrectly finding one of the comparisons significant. ANOVA guards against this inflation.

It is important to remember, however, that the results of an analysis of variance tell you about the overall or global status of differences among groups. If you find differences, ANOVA does not tell you which groups or pairs of groups are responsible. To get that information, you need to use post hoc comparisons such as Tukey's HSD (honestly significant difference) or Scheffé, Neuman-Keuls, or Dunnetts procedures. (More information on these techniques can be found in the appropriate sources listed in the "Suggested Readings" section.)

ANOVA is complex, and whole textbooks have been devoted to it. One-way ANOVAs are used in comparisons involving one factor or independent variable, and two-way ANOVAs are used for two factors. Example 4.4 displays a typical ANOVA table for a one-way analysis of variance.

ANOVA relies on the *F* distribution to test the hypothesis that the two variances are equal. The variation is divided into two components: the variation between each subject and the subjects' group mean (e.g., the variation between each participant in the experiment and the experimental group's mean) and the variation between each group mean and the grand mean (the mean of all groups). *The sum of squares, mean squares,* and *degrees of freedom* are all mathematical terms associated with ANOVA.

EXAMPLE 4.4
A Typical ANOVA Table

Source	Degrees of Freedom	Sum of Squares	Mean	F Ratio	p
Between groups					
Within groups					
Total					

Practical Significance:
Using Confidence Intervals

The results of a statistical analysis may be significant but not impressive enough to have practical applications. How can this be? Suppose that after an educational campaign in County A, children report a 10% increase in the use of bicycle helmets. In County B, the control, a 5% increase is reported, and the 5% difference between the two counties is statistically significant. Based on the results, you might be tempted to conclude that the educational campaign is effective. If, however, the expectation was that the campaign was to have reached at least 50% of County A's children, then the 10% achievement level is disappointing. You can conclude that the campaign, although "effective," is too weak to be continued or expanded. With very large samples, even small differences can be significant. When statistical significance alone is inadequate for the evaluation of your survey data, you should use confidence intervals. A **confidence interval** (CI) is the interval computed from sample data that has a given probability that the unknown parameter, such as the mean or proportion, is contained within the interval. Common confidence intervals are 90%, 95%, and 99%.

Suppose you conduct a survey with participants of Teach for the World, an international program aimed at encouraging the best teachers to participate in the education of children outside their own countries. Because of the complexity of the social and cultural issues involved, eligible teachers are assigned to Program 6, a relatively costly 6-month internship, or to Program 3, which requires only a 3-month internship. Of the 800 participants in Program 6, 480 (60%) respond well, as do 416 of the 800 (52%) in Program 3. Using a chi-square to assess the existence of a real difference between the two treatments, you obtain a p value of .001. This value is the probability of obtaining by chance the 8-point (60% – 52%) difference or an even larger difference between teachers in Program 6 and those in Program 3. The point estimate is 8 percentage points, but because of sampling and measurement errors (which always exist), the estimate is probably not identical to the true percentage difference between the two groups of teachers.

A confidence interval provides a plausible range for the true value. A CI is computed from sample data and has a given probability that the unknown true value is located within the interval. Using a standard method, the 95% CI of the 8-percentage-point difference comes out to be between 3% and 13%. A 95% CI means that about 95% of all such intervals would include the unknown true difference and 5% would not. Suppose, however, that, given the other costs of Program 6, the smallest practical and thus acceptable difference is 15%; then you can conclude that the 8-point difference between Programs 6 and 3 is not significant from a practical perspective, although it is statistically significant.

The confidence interval and p are related: If the interval contains 0 (no difference), then the p is not significant. However, if much of the interval is above the practical cutoff, then the results can be interpreted as practically inconclusive. For example, if the cutoff is 15% and the CI ranges from –1% to +25%, then much of the interval would fall above the cutoff for practical significance; the survey results would be unclear.

A graphic test for the differences between the means of two independent groups can also be prepared. In this method, the 95% CI is calculated and charted. If the means do *not* overlap, differences exist. If the mean of one group is contained in the interval of the second, differences do not exist. If the intervals overlap, but not the means, it is not possible to tell if differences exist, and a hypothesis test must be performed. Figure 4.1 shows how such charts can reveal differences in independent means.

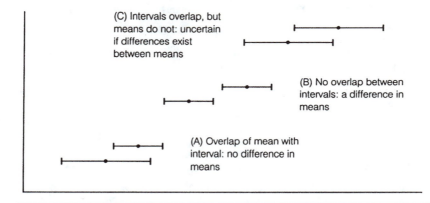

Figure 4.1. Using Confidence Intervals to Visualize Differences Between Independent Groups

EXERCISE

The following output was obtained from a survey to answer the question "How do Groups 1, 2, and 3 compare in their attitudes?" A score of 20 was the highest possible; high scores represented the most favorable attitudes.

a. What is the null hypothesis?
b. Chart the confidence intervals and tell if the differences among the groups are significant.
c. What is the *F* probability, and does it agree with the findings you obtained by representing the confidence intervals on a chart?

d. If you find significance, which of the three groups is likely to have contributed most to the finding?

| Page 2 | | | SPSS/PC+ | | | 12/15/93 |

- - - - - - - - - - - - O N E W A Y - - - - - - - - - - - -

| Variable | DV |
| by Variable | GROUP |

Analysis of Variance

Source	D.F.	Sum of Squares	Mean Squares	F Ratio	F Prob.
Between Groups	2	248.0000	124.0000	8.9793	.0020
Within Groups	18	248.5714	13.8095		
Total	20	496.5714			

- -

| Page 3 | | | SPSS/PC+ | | | 12/15/93 |

- - - - - - - - - - - - O N E W A Y - - - - - - - - - - - -

Group	Count	Mean	Standard Deviation	Standard Error	95 Pct Conf Int for Mean	
Grp 1	7	11.0000	3.6056	1.3628	7.6654 To	14.3346
Grp 2	7	8.1429	4.2984	1.6246	4.1675 To	12.1182
Grp 3	7	16.4286	3.1547	1.1924	13.5109 To	19.3462
Total	21	11.8571	4.9828	1.0873	9.5890 To	14.1253

Group	Minimum	Maximum
Grp 1	6.0000	16.0000
Grp 2	4.0000	13.0000
Grp 3	11.0000	19.0000
Total	4.0000	19.0000

- -

| Page 4 | | | SPSS/PC+ | | | 12/15/93 |

● ●

ANSWERS

a. The null hypothesis means that no differences in attitudes exist between the mean attitude scores of Groups 1, 2, and 3.

b.

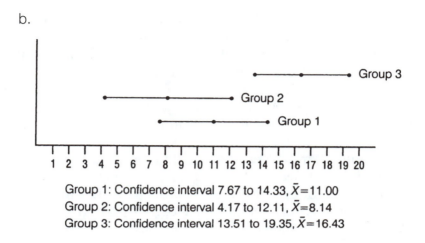

Group 1: Confidence interval 7.67 to 14.33, $\bar{X}$=11.00
Group 2: Confidence interval 4.17 to 12.11, $\bar{X}$=8.14
Group 3: Confidence interval 13.51 to 19.35, $\bar{X}$=16.43

Group 2's mean score is within Group 1's confidence interval. Group 3's interval does not overlap with either group. Statistically significant differences in the means can be seen, and so the null should be rejected.

c. The *F* probability is the observed significance level. It is smaller than the usual alphas (or critical values) of .05 or .01 and is statistically significant. The graphic and statistical tests agree.

d. ANOVA does not provide information about the group whose mean is responsible for the significant difference. The chart suggests that Group 3 is responsible.

Content Analysis of Qualitative Survey Data

Content analysis is a set of procedures used in the evaluation of qualitative information. This information may be collected directly (e.g., researchers may ask people questions about their knowledge, attitudes, and behavior) or indirectly (e.g., researchers may observe people's behavior). Perhaps the most familiar qualitative survey data come from responses to open-ended survey questions. Analyzing data from open-ended questions means poring over respondents' written or verbal comments to look for ideas or repeated themes. The ideas and themes found in the comments are then coded so that they can be counted and compared. Unlike the response choices found in statistical surveys, which are precoded, qualitative information is coded after it is collected.

Another familiar type of qualitative data comes from observations of people. For example, two members of a survey team might spend a month observing children on the playground to uncover patterns of play among girls and boys. The observers would then compare notes and summarize their findings.

Surveyors can also obtain qualitative data from documents and other media that were produced for other purposes. For instance, suppose you are interested in surveying changes over time in the news coverage of stories about the environment. Among the several types of news media available, you decide to restrict your survey to coverage found in local and national newspapers. As with any survey, you also have to be concerned about research design, sampling, and analysis. What time period should the review cover (10 years? 20 years?)? How many articles should you survey (all? a sample?)? How should you define and code each type of story? Which data-analytic methods are appropriate for you to use in comparing the numbers and types of stories over time? You might hypothesize that the numbers of newspaper stories about the environment increased significantly from 1980 to 1990, but that the numbers of stories from year to year have remained relatively constant since 1990. You can use content analysis methods, like statistical methods, to test these hypotheses and answer your research questions.

To conduct a content analysis, you need to undertake the following five activities:

1. Assemble the data from all sources.

2. Learn the contents of the data.

3. Create a codebook.

4. Enter and clean the data.

5. Do the analysis

ASSEMBLE THE DATA.

A survey database is a collection of information that is amenable to analysis. A qualitative survey can result in hundreds of pages of notes and transcripts. These unsorted data form the foundation of the qualitative survey database. They are not the same as the database, and, on their own, they are not interpretable or amenable to analysis.

The information collected in a qualitative survey takes the form of transcripts of interviews and focus group sessions; field notes from observations, interviews, and focus groups; responses to open-ended survey questions; and transcripts of written, spoken, and filmed materials.

Transcripts are printed accounts containing every word that was spoken or written during a survey. Producing a transcript can take a great deal of time. You can spend 4 or more hours producing a verbatim report of a typical discussion that took place during a 90-minute focus group with eight people, and the transcript may run to 50 or more pages of text.

Of course, not all data in a complete transcript are necessarily relevant, and producing complete transcripts may be unnecessary for most surveys. Sometimes people get sidetracked during discussions—they tell jokes, change the subject, and so on. Complete transcripts contain everything that was said, including such unrelated matters. Because producing complete transcripts is so time-consuming, and because such transcripts often contain a lot of material that is irrelevant to the survey topic, some surveyors prefer to produce abridged transcripts, which include all pertinent discussion and omit irrelevant remarks. If you use abridged transcripts, however, you should be aware that you run the risk of excluding important information. If someone other than you does the transcription, you need to make certain that he or she is trained in the nuances of the survey topic, so that no data are lost because they appeared unimportant to the transcriber.

Written transcripts cannot capture the expressions on people's faces during a discussion, nor can they adequately convey the passion with which some people state their positions. Because of this, surveyors often supplement transcripts with audio and visual documentation. Sometimes researchers use portions of these visual and audio records in their survey reports to illustrate their findings and lend a "human touch" to the reports' words and statistics. You should remember, however, that using your participants' words, voices, and visual images to justify or explain your findings or your viewpoint may raise legal and ethical questions, even if your survey is very small and you and the participants know one another. It is important that you give participants the opportunity to consent to the use of their words and visual images in the survey report and related materials in advance of data collection. You should provide them with information on where and under what circumstances the information will be used (if they consent) and what the risks and benefits to them are.

Field notes are the notes made by observers or interviewers "in the field," while they are conducting observations or interviews. Sorting through and transcribing field notes is an onerous process. The persons who took the notes must review them and fill in any blanks, and this requires that they remember what was said and done, when, and by whom. Some people have great memories; others are less fortunate. Some take better notes than others.

It is preferable to have two or more people taking notes in the field, so that their findings can be compared and interrater reliability can be estimated. Having two or more note takers or observers may also reduce the amount of recall needed to assemble a complete set of data. If one observer has not noted or has forgotten who did what to whom, perhaps another has recorded the information in great detail.

But this is an expensive process that increases the personnel costs of the survey. Also, with two or more people taking notes, you can expect disagreements, and disagreements are typically arbitrated by a third person, which also increases the time and expense of organizing notes and observations.

Focus groups are targeted discussion groups. To be effective, a focus group must have a skilled moderator, one who is able to focus the group members' attention on a specific topic. The discussions in focus groups are often recorded by note-taking observers because the group moderators are too busy leading the discussions to keep accurate records. Even skilled note takers, however, may leave much information out due to the difficulty of capturing all of the points made by every speaker. Because researchers fear losing vital information, focus groups are usually at least audiotaped; when possible, they are videotaped. Voice recognition software is now available that may become part of the focus group leader's toolbox, eliminating some of the difficulties caused by the need to transcribe or interpret notes. (For more on focus groups, see **How to Ask Survey Questions,** Volume 2 in this series.)

Qualitative data also come from responses to open-ended questions, which are often included in even highly structured surveys. Open-ended questions are considered essential to any survey, because it is often important to let people have their say in their own words. Example 4.5 shows how open-ended questions are typically used in structured surveys.

EXAMPLE 4.5
Qualitative Data From Open-Ended Questions

1. How would you rate your experience with customer service for Esale.com?

   Excellent ....❏

   Very good ....❏

   Good ....❏

   Fair ....❏

   Unacceptable ....❏

2. What was the main reason you contacted customer service?

   _____

   _____

   _____

   _____

3. Please feel free to comment on any aspect of your experience with Esale.com or with this survey.

   _____

   _____

   _____

   _____

Little evidence is currently available concerning the effects of open-ended questions on the accuracy or usefulness of statistical surveys. Some surveyors who include open-ended questions read every word of every response and try to address every issue raised by respondents. This tends to be true of researchers conducting relatively small surveys. Other surveyors suggest that, on average, only extremely satisfied or extremely dissatisfied people bother to comment when invited to, so their comments are not very useful because they do not apply to the average or typical respondent. Some surveyors even suggest that open-ended questions are not necessary in really good survey instruments because such instruments already include in the questions and response choices everything the surveyor needs to know.

At their best, responses to open-ended questions can provide you with information that was not revealed in the focus groups, cognitive tests, or pilot tests you conducted before you administered the final survey instrument. But beware of hoping for too much from open-ended questions—the responses you get may be difficult to read or understand because they are illegible or incoherent, or they may raise issues about which you can do little or nothing, and your failure to act may be frustrating for respondents.

LEARN THE CONTENTS OF THE DATA

The second step in conducting a content analysis is to become extremely familiar with the data you have collected. You must understand the data before you can assign codes to them in anticipation of data entry and analysis. Learning the contents of the data can mean reading through hundreds of recorded pages of text and watching videotapes or listening to audiotapes for days or weeks. Even if all of your data come from one focus group, you may find yourself spending at least a day reacquainting yourself with the discussion and 4 to 8 hours transcribing an hour's worth of tape.

CREATE A CODEBOOK

When your survey uses closed-ended questions, you assign codes or values to responses in advance of data collection. When your survey uses open-ended questions, you cannot assign codes until after the data are collected. Example 4.6 illustrates coding for both kinds of questions.

EXAMPLE 4.6
Coding Closed- and Open-Ended Questions

Closed-Ended Questions

The following are excerpts from a survey concerning visits to a clinic made by new mothers in a experimental program to prevent fetal alcohol syndrome.

Question 5. Did the mother visit the clinic within 2 weeks of delivery? (postpartum)

Yes   (1)
No   (2)
No data   (9)

Question 7. Did the mother visit the clinic within 6 weeks of delivery? (well visit)

Yes   (1)
No   (2)
No data   (9)

A corresponding portion of the codebook for this survey looks like this:

Example 4.6 continued

Variable Number	Label	Description and Comments
1	PROJID	A five-digit ID project code
		Use 99999 for missing values.
2	INDIVID	A four-digit ID individual code
		Use 9999 for missing values.
3	DLIVDATE	Enter month/day/year using 2 digits for each segment. Example: May 20, 2002 = 052002.
		Use 99 for any missing segment.
		Use 999999 if entire date is missing.
4	FOLLDATE	Use same procedure as for DLIVDATE.
5	POSPARVIS	No = 1, Yes = 2, Don't know = 3
		Use 9 if missing.
6	VISTDATE	Follow DLIVDATE PROCEDURE.
		If POSTPARTUM VISIT = No, use 888888; use 999999 if missing.
7	WELVISIT	Use 2 digits: No = 01, Yes = 02
		Use 00 if none; 99 if missing.

Open-Ended Questions

The following are excerpts from summarized transcripts from a focus group conducted to ascertain knowledge of and attitudes toward depression among uninsured adults.

Example 4.6 continued

Theme	Code
Knowledge of and attitudes toward depression	1
Identified common depressive symptoms but did not always conceptualize them as an illness	1
Acknowledged role of environmental stress	1
Knowledge and attitudes toward counseling	2
Wanted to help themselves but felt impaired by depression and lack of information	2
Felt that having someone to talk to in a confidential manner, to be able to "unburden oneself," would be helpful	2
Believed counselor might be able to help them solve their own problems, change their negative thoughts and behaviors, have a more positive outlook	2

ENTER AND CLEAN THE DATA

Data entry consists of organizing and storing the contents of transcripts and notes. Data may be entered and organized in many different ways—by person, place, observation, quotation, and so on. For a very small survey, you might organize your data onto index cards. Other options for organizing your data include spreadsheet programs, database management programs, and word processing programs.

Special software for qualitative analysis is also available, including a program offered free by the Centers for Disease Control (at www.cdc.gov; click on "software"). CDC EZ-Text is a software program designed to assist researchers in creating, managing, and analyzing qualitative data gathered through semistructured interviews. Using this software, you can design a series of data entry templates tailored to your survey. You can enter a response to a question into EZ-Text either as a verbatim transcript (e.g., from a tape recording) or as a summary generated from the interviewer's notes. You can type data from respondents directly into the templates or copy data from word processor documents. Following data entry, you can interactively create online codebooks, apply codes to specific response passages, develop case studies, conduct database searches to identify text passages that meet particular conditions that you specify, and export data in a wide array of formats for further analysis with other qualitative or statistical analysis software programs. EZ-Text also enables you to calculate coder reliability statistics. If your survey is being conducted in several sites, the manager at each one can merge data files for combined cross-site analyses.

Cleaning the data may include making decisions about which data to discard. Why would anyone ever discard data? You may have to discard some if they are indecipherable (e.g., your notes are incomplete or unreadable and the audiotape broke) or irrelevant. If you decide to discard any data, you must create rules regarding what you will do about lost or missing data. How much effect will missing data have on the conclusions you can draw? If you do have data missing, you need to be sure to discuss the implications of this in your survey report. (For more on cleaning the data, see Chapter 1.)

Once you have cleaned the data and you understand their strengths and weaknesses, you can organize them into a database. Only a clean database stands a chance of producing reliable information. Inconsistent and incomprehensible information is invalid. Obtaining a clean database is an objective shared by qualitative and statistical survey researchers. It requires time to do well, and you should include data entry and cleaning as major tasks in the planning of all surveys, regardless of their size.

DO THE ANALYSIS

The final step in conducting a content analysis is the actual analysis itself. The analysis may be inductive or deductive. In an inductive analysis, you go through the data and look for dominant themes. For example, in ethnographic research you might use inductive analysis to put forward theories to explain culture, values, and behavior.

Consider the themes and subthemes shown in Example 4.7, which have been identified by a researcher who has reviewed transcripts of an interviewer's discussions with second- and third-generation immigrants from Korea, Japan, and India. The transcripts take two forms: written (85 pages) and tape-recorded (8 hours). The example shows that the researcher has identified four themes, each of which has two subthemes. Compared with the themes, the subthemes enable the researcher to be more specific about the respondents' histories, values, conflicts, and identities. That is, by identifying subthemes, the researcher can tell that the respondents are concerned about values, particularly respect for elders and the relationship between community and individual rights.

EXAMPLE 4.7
Themes and Subthemes Evoked by a Review of Hypothetical Transcripts of Interviews With Second- and Third-Generation Americans

Themes	Subthemes
History	Religion
	Social mores such as food, clothing
Values	Respect for elders
	Community versus individual rights
Conflicts	Generations
	Cultures
Identity	American versus Korean, Japanese, Indian
	Korean, Japanese, Indian versus American

In a deductive analysis, you start with preselected themes and subthemes derived from the research literature and your own experience. You then comb through the data and count every instance of support for your themes and subthemes. Example 4.8 shows how a deductive analysis might work.

EXAMPLE 4.8
Barriers to After-School Parenting Classes

Survey: Interviews with 200 teen parents in 10 schools

Purpose: To discover barriers to attendance at parenting classes

Premise: Barriers include lack of transportation, lack of child care, inability to take time off from work, lack of motivation (don't think they need the classes)

Question: Which of the following is the most important reason you or other teen parents might not be able to attend parenting classes? [The barriers are listed.]

Analysis: Count each time a particular barrier (e.g., lack of transportation) is chosen as the most important reason

Results:

	Males (*n* = 50)	Females (*n* = 150)
Lack of transportation	15	56
Lack of child care	0	61
Inability to take time off from work	10	17
Don't need classes	25	16

In a content analysis, you group the ideas put forth by participants and code similar ideas identically. You can then analyze the information in several different ways. For example, you can count the frequency with which an idea is repeated, or you can compare the number of times men come up with an idea with the number of times women do (as shown in Example 4.8). Unlike the analysis plans for statistical surveys, analysis plans for qualitative surveys are often created after the fact—that is, after the data are collected. (For more on analysis plans, see Chapter 1.)

RELATIONAL DATABASES

Many researchers who are responsible for large surveys have found that relational database management software programs are extremely useful for qualitative data management. In a **relational database**, you create data tables that are linked (related) by primary codes, such as individuals' ID numbers. The tables look very much like single spreadsheets, each with one person's data entered across the rows of the table and each of the variables (e.g., age, comments on an issue) listed down the columns.

Suppose the Nikko Running Shoe Company wants to survey its customers. The survey's purposes are to find out customer preferences in a running shoe and how Nikko can improve its image among customers. Nikko's survey team uses a program such as Microsoft Access to create three tables. The first table lists the names of all of Nikko's customers along with their addresses and their previous orders. In the second table, the team lists the demographics and other personal characteristics of each customer, including where each lives and how much he or she runs each week. The third table contains responses to two previous Nikko surveys on running shoes. Key identifiers—that is, the customers' ID numbers—link the tables. Information stored in this format enables Nikko's survey team to conduct surveys of customers in certain parts of the country who have ordered running shoes at least three times in the past 2 years and who have completed surveys in the past year. For instance, the team can use the database to describe the demographic characteristics of Nikko's customers in New York and Los Angeles who were least satisfied with their purchases and give the reasons for their dissatisfaction. The survey team can even import the database into ASCII text files and spreadsheets, which they can then import into data analysis programs.

Analysis of Open-Ended Questions: Best and Least Liked

A very common use of surveys is to find out if people are satisfied with new products, services, or programs. Their opinions provide important insights into why new ideas or new ways of doing things do or do not get adopted. One kind of set of open-ended questions that is particularly appropriate for determining satisfaction involves the collection of information about what people like best (LB) about a product or service and what they like least (LL). To use the LB/LL method, follow the three steps described below.

Step 1. Ask respondents to list what is good and what is bad. Always set a limit on the number of responses; for example, "Name at least one thing, but no more than three things, you like best about your participation in the focus group." If respondents cannot come up with three responses to such a request, they can leave blank spaces or write "none." If they give more than three, you can keep or discard the extras, depending on the information you need.

You may want to focus on some particular aspect of your subject of interest, instead of asking about the entire product or service; for example, "Name at least one thing, but no more than three things, you like best about the instructional materials handed out before the focus group discussion."

Step 2. Categorize and code all the responses. You can create categories based on your review of the responses or based on your past experience with similar services, products, or activities.

Try to keep the categories as precise as possible—that is, opt for more rather than fewer—because you will find it easier to combine small categories later, if necessary, than to break up large categories.

Suppose that focus group participants gave the following answers to the question on what they liked least about the activity:

- Some people did all the talking.

- The leader didn't always listen.

- I couldn't say anything without being interrupted.

- Too much noise and confusion.

- Some members of the group were ignored.

- The leader didn't take control.

- I didn't get a chance to say anything.

- Meles and Petrus were the only ones who talked.

- The leader didn't seem to care.

- I couldn't hear myself think.

You might categorize and code these answers as shown in Example 4.9, and then match your codes and the responses as shown in Example 4.10.

EXAMPLE 4.9
Response Categories

Category	Code
Leader didn't listen (ignored participants; didn't seem to care)	1
Some people monopolized discussion (did all the talking; couldn't say anything; Meles and Petrus were the only ones who talked)	2
Disorderly environment (too much noise; leader didn't take control; couldn't hear myself think)	3

EXAMPLE 4.10
Group Member Responses

Response	Code
Member A	
The instructor didn't always listen.	1
I couldn't hear myself think.	3
I couldn't say anything without being interrupted.	2
Member B	
The leader didn't always listen.	1
The leader didn't take control when things got noisy.	3
The leader ignored some participants.	3
Member C	
I didn't get a chance to say anything.	2

To make sure you have assigned the codes correctly, you should establish their reliability by bringing in another rater and finding out if the two of you agree. In other words, are the ratings reliable? If not, negotiate the differences or redo the codes.

Step 3. When you are satisfied about the reliability of your ratings, the next step is to count the number of responses for each code. Example 4.11 shows how you would do this for 10 focus group participants. Look at the number of responses in each category. The 10 focus group members listed 30 things they liked least about the discussion group. Of the 30, 17 (more than 50%) were assigned to the same category, Code 2, and you could justly argue that, based on the data, what the participants tended to like least about the focus group was that some people monopolized the discussion and others did not get a chance to say anything.

EXAMPLE 4.11
Number of Responses for Each Code

Participant	Codes			Total
	1	2	3	
A	1	1	1	3
B	1	—	2	3
C		2	1	3
D		1	2	3
E		3	—	3
F		2	1	3
G		2	1	3
H		2	1	3
I		3	2	5
J		1	—	1

Next, count the *number* of participants whose answers are assigned to each code—for example, only Participants A and B gave answers that are coded 1 (see Example 4.12). Look at the number of focus group participants whose responses fit each category. Because 8 or 9 of the 10 participants gave responses that fell into the same categories (Codes 2 and 3), their opinions probably represent those of the entire group. It is safe to add that the participants also disliked the disorderly atmosphere that prevailed during the focus group. They complained that the noise made it hard to think clearly and that the leader did not take control.

EXAMPLE 4.12
Participants' Response Pattern

Code	Number of Participants Listing a Response Assigned to This Code	Which Participants?
1	2	A and B
2	9	All but B
3	8	All but E and I

When respondents agree with one another, there will be few types of answers, and many people will list them. If respondents disagree, many different kinds of answers will turn up on their lists, and only a few people (less than 10%) will be associated with each type.

Interpreting LB/LL data gets more complex when you have many participants and responses to categorize. Suppose, for example, you asked 100 students to indicate which aspects of a health education program they like best. First, you must decide on your response categories and assign each one a code. Then try this:

1. Put the codes in rank order. That is, if the largest number of students chose responses that are assigned to Code 3, list Code 3 first.

2. Calculate the percentage of students assigned to each code. If 40 of 100 students chose responses that were assigned to Code 3, then the calculation would be 40%.

3. Count the number of responses assigned to each code.

4. Calculate the percentage of responses assigned to each code. If 117 responses from a total of 400 were assigned to Code 3, then 29.25% (117/400) of responses were for Code 3.

5. Calculate the cumulative percentage of response by adding the percentages together: 29.25% + 20.25% = 49.50%.

The table in Example 4.13 summarizes these steps with some hypothetical survey data. Among other things, this table tells us the following:

- The highest numbers and percentages of participants and responses were assigned to Code 3, followed by responses assigned to Code 4.

- Nearly 50% of all responses (49.50%) were assigned to Codes 3 and 4.

- Of the 10 coded response categories, more than three-fourths (77.75%) were encompassed by 4 codes: 3, 4, 7, and 8.

- Five codes—3, 4, 7, 8, and 10—accounted for nearly all responses (92.50%).

EXAMPLE 4.13
Summary of Responses

Response Categories (codes arranged in rank order)	% of 100 Participants Assigned to Each Code	No. of 400 Responses Assigned to Each Code	% of Responses Assigned to Each Code	Cumulative % of Responses Assigned to Each Code
3	40	117	29.25	29.25
4	34	81	20.25	49.50
7	32	78	19.50	69.00
8	20	35	8.75	77.75
10	17	30	7.50	85.25
1	15	29	7.25	92.50
6	10	14	3.50	96.00
2	5	10	2.50	98.50
9	3	5	1.25	99.75
5	1	1	0.25	100

Exercises

1. Indicate the type of data likely to be obtained for each of the following:

    a. Ethnicity
    b. Date of birth
    c. Ratings of happiness on a scale from 1 to 5
    d. Preferences

2. Compute the mean, median, and mode for the results of a survey of U.S. eating preferences for Christmas dinner.

First Choice	Number of Respondents
Turkey	10
Prime rib	9
Ham	6
Lamb	4
Vegetarian	3
Goose	2
Other (e.g., steak)	1

3. A mail survey with 75 respondents yielded a mean score of 100 and a range of 100 (minimum, 50; maximum, 150). An additional questionnaire with a score of 100 was mailed in after the analysis had been completed. Redo the analysis and report on the mean, range, and sample size.

4. Indicate if each of the following is true or false.

Statement	True?	False?
The sample size has an influence on whether a difference in means is found.		
The obtained p for a t test is the probability that the means of two groups are the same.		
If the obtained p is very large, the means of the two groups are equal.		
The independent t test is less sensitive to differences than the paired t test.		
The p is calculated before alpha.		
If group sample sizes are equal, unequal variances do *not* cause major problems in the t test.		
If group sample sizes are equal, unequal variances do *not* cause major problems in analysis of variance (ANOVA).		

5. For each of the following situations, describe the independent and dependent variables and tell whether they will be described with nominal, ordinal, or numerical data.

Situation	Describe Independent and Dependent Variables	Are Data Nominal, Ordinal, or Numerical?
Patients in the experimental and control groups tell whether painkillers give complete, moderate, or very little relief.		
Participants are divided into four groups: very tall, tall, short, very short. All are surveyed regarding their self-esteem, with a score of 1 meaning very low self-esteem and 9 meaning very high self-esteem.		
Residents of a facility are chosen according to whether they have had all recommended vaccinations or not; they are followed for 5 years, and their health status is monitored.		
Men and women with Stage 1, 2, and 3 disease are compared on quality of life, as measured by scores ranging from 1 to 50.		
Customers of two catalog companies are surveyed, and their average scores are compared.		

6. Use the following information to select and justify a method of data analysis.

   Question: Does program participation improve participants' ability to be good parents?

   Standard: A statistically significant difference in ability is found between families that have participated in the experimental program and families in the control program.

   Independent Variable: Group membership (experimental versus control)

   Design: An experimental design with concurrent controls (eligible participants assigned at random to the experimental and control groups)

   Sampling: 100 participants in each group (a statistically derived sample size)

   Dependent Variable: Ability to be a good parent

   Type(s) of Data: One important measure is the PARENT, a 50-point survey in which higher scores mean better parents.

   Analytic method: [fill in]

7. Suppose the survey of the effectiveness of a program to help improve ability to be a parent is concerned with finding out how younger and older persons compare in the experimental and control groups. Assuming the use of the PARENT survey, which produces numerical scores, which statistical method would be appropriate? Explain.

ANSWERS

1. a. Nominal

   b. Numerical

   c. Ordinal

   d. Not enough information to tell. If scores, then numerical; ratings, ordinal; yes or no to a list, nominal.

2. Turkey is the mode; data are nominal, so you cannot compute the median or mean.

3. The mean and range stay the same. The sample size increases from 75 to 76.

4.

Statement	True?	False?
The sample size has an influence on whether a difference in means is found.	X	
The obtained p for a t test is the probability that the means of two groups are the same.		X
If the obtained p is very large, the means of the two groups are equal.		X
The independent t test is less sensitive to differences than the paired t test.		X
The p is calculated before alpha.	X	
If group sample sizes are equal, unequal variances do *not* cause major problems in the t test.	X	
If group sample sizes are equal, unequal variances do *not* cause major problems in analysis of variance (ANOVA).		X

5.

Situation	Describe Independent and Dependent Variables	Are Data Nominal, Ordinal, or Numerical?
Patients in the experimental and control groups tell whether painkillers give complete, moderate, or very little relief.	Independent variable: group Dependent variable: pain relief	Independent variable is nominal; dependent variable is ordinal.
Participants are divided into four groups: very tall, tall, short, very short. All are surveyed regarding their self-esteem, with a score of 1 meaning very low self-esteem and 9 meaning very high self-esteem.	Independent variable: height Dependent variable: self-esteem	Independent variable is ordinal; dependent variable is numerical.
Residents of a facility are chosen according to whether they have had all recommended vaccinations or not; they are followed for 5 years, and their health status is monitored.	Independent variable: having or not having recommended vaccinations Dependent variable: health status	Independent variable is nominal; there is not enough information to determine the dependent variable.
Men and women with Stage 1, 2, and 3 disease are compared on quality of life, as measured by scores ranging from 1 to 50.	Independent variable: gender and stage of disease Dependent variable: quality of life	Independent variables are nominal and ordinal; dependent variable is numerical.
Customers of two catalog companies are surveyed, and their average scores are compared.	Independent variable: catalog company Dependent variable: satisfaction	Independent variable is nominal; dependent variable is numerical.

6. *Analysis:* A two-sample independent groups *t* test

   Justification for the Analysis: This *t* test is appropriate when the independent variable is

measured on a categorical scale and the dependent variable is measured on a numerical scale. In this case, the assumptions of a *t* test are met. These assumptions are that each group is normally distributed (or has a sample size of at least 30) and that group variances are equal.

7. If the survey's aim is to find out how younger and older persons in the experimental and control groups compare in ability to be good parents, and assuming that the statistical assumptions are met, then analysis of variance is an appropriate technique.

Suggested Readings

Afifi, A. A., & Clark, V. A. (1990). *Computer-aided multivariate analysis.* New York: Van Nostrand Reinhold.

Textbook on multivariate analysis with a practical approach. Discusses data entry, data screening, data reduction, and data analysis. Also explains the options available in different statistical packages.

Bourque, L. B., & Clark V. A. (1992). *Processing data: The survey example.* Newbury Park, CA: Sage.

Excellent source of information about the complexities of data processing. Gives many examples.

Braitman, L. (1991). Confidence intervals assess both clinical and statistical significance. *Annals of Internal Medicine, 114,* 515-517.

Contains one of the clearest explanations anywhere of the use of confidence intervals; highly recommended.

Dawson, B., & Trapp, R. G. (2000). *Basic and clinical biostatistics* (3rd ed.). New York: McGraw-Hill.

Basic and essential primer on the use of statistics in medicine and medical care settings. Explains study designs and how to summarize and present data; discusses sampling and the main statistical methods used in analyzing data.

Field Institute. (2002). *The Field Poll.* Online at www.field.com/fieldpoll.

Web site of the Field Institute, a public opinion news service with more than 2,000 polls to its credit, provides access to sample polls and to codebooks that include explanations of sampling strategies and designs. Excellent examples of how public opinion polls actually look in practice.

Fink, A. (1993). *Evaluation fundamentals: Guiding health programs, research, and policy.* Newbury Park, CA: Sage.

Chapter 7 discusses basic statistical methods. Examples and exercises are tailored to program evaluation, but many are applicable to surveys in general because survey data are often used in evaluation studies.

Fink, A., Hays, R. D., Moore, A. A., & Beck, J. C. (1996). Alcohol-related problems in the elderly: Determinants, consequences and screening. *Archives of Internal Medicine, 156,* 1150-1156.

Literature review provides a good example of a content analysis.

Hegland, S. (2002). *Research methods in human development and family studies handbook.* Online at www.public.iastate.edu/~shegland (click on "HD FS 503," then click on "Handbook").

Handbook (prepared for use by students taking the author's courses) provides an overview of research methods, including data analysis. Section on content analysis may be of special interest.

Siegel, S. (1956). *Nonparametric statistics for the behavioral sciences.* New York: McGraw-Hill.

Classic textbook on nonparametric statistics.

Thompson, K. M., & Haninger, K. (2001). Violence in e-rated video games. *Journal of the American Medical Association, 286,* 591-598.

Excellent example of a content analysis in action for an important public health problem. Available online at jama.ama-assn.org/issues/v286n5/abs/jtv10003.html.

Statistica. (2002). *Electronic statistics textbook.* Online at statsoftinc.com/textbook/stathome.html

Covers everything a good statistics text covers and then some; includes an excellent glossary. Highly recommended for those interested in learning about statistics as well as those who want to learn statistics.

Trochim, W. M. K. (2000). *The research methods knowledge base* (2nd ed.). Cincinnati, OH: Atomic Dog.

Comprehensive textbook (available online at trochim.human.cornell.edu/kb) that addresses all of the topics in a typical introductory undergraduate or graduate course in social research methods. Covers the entire research process, including data management (a brief discussion) and data analysis.

Glossary

Alpha—The probability of rejecting the null hypothesis when it is actually true.

Alternative hypothesis (H_1)—A statement that disagrees with the null hypothesis, asserting that a difference exists and in which direction. Also called *research hypothesis.*

Analysis of variance (ANOVA)—A statistical procedure used to determine whether or not there are any differences among two or more groups of respondents on one or more factors. The *F* test is used in ANOVA.

Analysis plan—A plan concerning the analyses to be performed for each main survey objective, hypothesis, or research question.

Chi-square test—The statistical test used to test the null hypothesis that the proportions are equal or that factors or characteristics are independent or not associated.

Codebook—A survey project's official record; contains the survey instrument (including the scoring system, if relevant); the variable names, labels, and values or codes; the locations of codes in the data file; information on survey methods and findings; and the names of all survey team members.

133

Codes—The units or symbols that computer programs use to identify variables.

Confidence interval—The interval computed from sample data that has a given probability that the unknown parameter, such as the mean or proportion, is contained within the interval. Common confidence intervals are 90%, 95%, and 99%.

Content analysis—A method for analyzing and interpreting qualitative survey data, which is collected directly or indirectly through interviews, observations, and examinations of writings, films, and recordings.

Correlation analysis—Analysis that is concerned with the relationship between two variables.

Correlation coefficient—A measure of a straight-line, or linear, relationship between two variables.

Curvilinear relationship—The kind of relationship that exists if the distribution of data for either the independent or the dependent variable is skewed or contains outlying values.

Data entry—The process of transcribing survey data into a database. The data may be entered directly into a database management or spreadsheet program, entered directly or indirectly into a statistical program, or scanned.

Data management—The organization of survey information so that it can be analyzed.

Dependent variables—The responses to, outcomes of, or results of interventions.

Descriptive statistics—Statistics that describe data in terms of measures of central tendency.

Dichotomous variables—Variables that are divided into two components (e.g., 12 years of age and younger or 13 years of age and older; score of 0 to 50 or 51 and older;

read five books or more in past month or read four or fewer).

Distribution—An arrangement of data that shows the frequency of occurrence of the values (e.g., scores and other numerical values, such as number of years in office, age in years as of today) of a variable or characteristic (e.g., attitudes, knowledge, behavior, health status, and demographics, such as age, income).

Expected value—The mean of a sampling distribution.

Field notes—Notes made by observers or interviewers "in the field," while they are conducting observations or interviews.

Focus group—A carefully selected group of people who are brought together to give their opinions and offer their perspectives on specific topics.

Imputation—A method of estimating how respondents might have answered unanswered survey questions. Answers are imputed based on assumptions about how respondents with missing data compare with other respondents.

Independent variables (or explanatory or predictor variables)—Variables used to explain or predict a response, outcome, or result (the dependent variable).

Interquartile range—The difference between the 25th and 75th percentiles; contains 50% of the observations.

Kappa—A statistic that is used to measure how much better than chance the agreement is between a pair of coders on the presence or absence of yes/no themes in texts.

Mean—The arithmetic average of observations.

Measures of central tendency—Measures or statistics that describe the location of the center of a distribution; these are the mean, median, and mode.

Measures of dispersion—Descriptive statistics that depict the spread of numerical data; these are the range, standard deviation, and percentiles.

Median—The middle observation; half of the observations are smaller and half are larger.

Missing data—Incomplete information due to unanswered questions on survey instruments or lost questionnaires.

Mode of a distribution—The value of the observations that occurs most frequently.

Nominal scale—A scale that has no numerical values and produces data that fit into categories, such as country of birth or gender.

Normal distribution—A distribution that takes the form of a smooth, bell-shaped curve that is continuous and symmetric around the mean, which is symbolized by μ (Greek letter mu).

Null hypothesis (H_o)—A statement that no difference exists between the averages or mean scores of two groups.

Numerical scale—A scale on which differences between numbers have a meaning. Age is a numerical variable, and so are weight and length of survival after diagnosis of a serious disease.

Odds ratio—An estimate of the relative risk calculated in case-control studies. It is the odds that a respondent was exposed to a given risk factor divided by the odds that a control was exposed to the risk factor.

One-tailed hypothesis test—A test in which the alternative hypothesis specifies a deviation from the null hypothesis in one direction only. The rejection region is located on one end of the distribution of the test statistic.

Ordinal scale—A scale that provides respondents with choices that have an inherent order.

Outlier—A respondent who provides observations that appear to be inconsistent with the rest of the data set.

***p* value**—The probability that an observed result (or result of a statistical test) is due to chance rather than to participation in a program (or exposure to some other innovation or intervention). The probability is calculated after the statistical test.

Percentage—A form of proportion in which the part of the whole is expressed in hundredths.

Percentile—A number that indicates the percentage of a distribution that is equal to or below that number.

Proportion—The number of observations or responses with a given characteristic divided by the total number of observations.

Range—The difference between the largest observation and the smallest.

Rate—A form of proportion measured per unit of some multiplier or base, such as 1,000, 10,000, or 100,000. Rates are always computed over time (e.g., over the course of a year).

Ratio—The relationship of one *part* of the whole to another *part,* expressed as a part divided by another part, for example, the number of observations in a given group with a certain characteristic (e.g., feeling better) divided by the number of observations without the given characteristic (e.g., feeling worse).

Regression analysis—A form of analysis that is used to predict values. It involves estimating the components of a mathematical model that reflects the relationship between the dependent and independent variables in the population.

Relational databases—Data tables that are linked (related) by primary codes, such as individual respondents' ID numbers.

Relationship—A consistent association between or among variables.

GLOSSARY

Research hypothesis—See **Alternative hypothesis (H_1)**

Sampling distribution—The distribution of a test statistic, such as the mean, t, F, and chi-square.

Skewed distribution—A distribution that has a few outlying observations—a few small values or a few large ones—in one direction.

Spearman rank correlation (or Spearman's rho)—Describes the relationship between two ordinal characteristics or one ordinal and one numerical characteristic.

Standard deviation—A common measure of the dispersion or spread of the data around the mean.

Standard error—The variability in a sampling distribution.

Statistics—The mathematics of organizing and interpreting numerical information.

Survey—A system for collecting information from or about people in order to describe, compare, or explain their knowledge, attitudes, and behavior.

Symmetric distribution—A distribution that has the same shape on both sides of the mean.

Transcript—A printed account containing every word that was spoken or written during a survey.

Transformation of data—Manipulation of the data so as to change the scale of measurement.

t test—The statistical test for comparing a mean with a norm or for comparing two means with small sample sizes (fewer than 30).

Two-tailed hypothesis test—A test in which the alternative hypothesis specifies a deviation from the null hypothesis in either direction. The rejection region is located in both ends of the distribution of the test statistic.

Variable—A measurable characteristic that varies in a population.

Weighting—A statistical method that is used to make up for nonresponse. For example, if you expect that your survey will be completed by a sample made up of 50% men and 50% women, but only 40% of the completed surveys are returned by men, you can weight the men's returns so that they are equivalent to 50%.

About the Author

Arlene Fink, Ph.D., is Professor of Medicine and Public Health at the University of California, Los Angeles. She is on the Policy Advisory Board of UCLA's Robert Wood Johnson Clinical Scholars Program, a consultant to the UCLA-Neuropsychiatric Institute Health Services Research Center, and President of Arlene Fink Associates, a research and evaluation company. She has conducted surveys and evaluations throughout the United States and abroad and has trained thousands of health professionals, social scientists, and educators in survey research, program evaluation, and outcomes and effectiveness research. Her published works include more than 100 articles, books, and monographs. She is co-author of *How to Conduct Surveys: A Step-by-Step Guide* and author of *Evaluation Fundamentals: Guiding Health Programs, Research, and Policy; Evaluation for Education and Psychology;* and *Conducting Literature Reviews: From Paper to the Internet.*